blue
rider
press

SOUND MAN

SOUND MAN

Glyn Johns

BLUE RIDER PRESS
a member of Penguin Group (USA)
New York

blue
rider
press

Published by the Penguin Group
Penguin Group (USA) LLC
375 Hudson Street
New York, New York 10014

USA · Canada · UK · Ireland · Australia
New Zealand · India · South Africa · China

penguin.com
A Penguin Random House Company

Sections from *Stones European Tour, Spring 1957* previously published in *stu* by misc;
© 2003 by Out-Take Ltd.

Library of Congress Cataloging-in-Publication Data

Johns, Glyn, date.
Sound man / Glyn Johns.
p.   cm.
ISBN 978-0-399-16387-6
1. Johns, Glyn, 1942–   2. Sound recording executives and
producers—United States—Biography.   I. Title.
ML429.J636A3   2014   2014027145
781.49092—dc23
[B]

Printed in the United States of America
1   3   5   7   9   10   8   6   4   2

BOOK DESIGN BY AMANDA DEWEY

For Dilys and Christopher

CONTENTS

SOUND MAN

PREFACE

Someone asked me the other day: What exactly does a record producer do? My answer was: "You just have to have an opinion and the ego to express it more convincingly than anyone else." Every time I start another project I wonder if I am going to get found out.

So much of what any of us achieve in life has a massive element of good fortune attached. In my case, you can start with being born in 1942, which tipped me out into the workplace just as things were getting interesting in the music business, along with a whole host of artists who were to change the face of popular music. They were to drag me with them on the crest of a wave through an extraordinary period of change, not only in the music they were writing and performing but in the structure of the industry itself. Every now and then, when the opportunity presented itself, I would try to "express my opinion more convincingly than anyone else," and there were a few who took notice.

I started working as a recording engineer in 1959, just before the demise of the 78. It was the beginning of the vinyl age. Mono was the thing and stereo was only for hi-fi freaks.

Bill Haley and His Comets had started the American rock and roll invasion in Britain in the mid-fifties, and it had been rammed home by Elvis, Fats Domino, Jerry Lee Lewis, and Chuck Berry, to name but a few. They dominated the charts in the UK, along with ballad singers like Doris Day, Tony Bennett, and Perry Como. British artists were just copying whatever was arriving from across the pond, even singing with an American accent. There had not as yet been a homegrown response. Music was still extremely safe and somewhat insipid in comparison to what was to follow.

The record industry as we know it now was in its infancy. In England they were grappling with the trickle before the floodgate opened to the changes that were about to take place. Those in charge had no concept of what was about to happen and most certainly did not lead the way. As a result, some of them fell by the wayside, others were led by the nose, and some were clever enough to sit back, keep quiet, and allow themselves to be carried through the next few years by the explosion of youth that was to take over.

The ensuing years were full of excitement, much adrenaline, many dawn choruses, and extremes of every emotion you can imagine. I was blasted through my youth into middle age with an extraordinary combination of creative people, sounds, rhythm, and lyrics in a period of time that I believe is unlikely to ever be repeated. I have been extremely fortunate in witnessing firsthand some wonderful moments with some truly fantastic, innovative artists while making records as an engineer and producer over the last fifty years, and watching the creative process change into something almost un-recognizable from where I started. All this while plowing my way through the minefield of "the business" and the incredible cast of characters it threw up—managers, lawyers, entrepreneurs, promoters, publishers, and so-called executives, large and small.

AT IBC STUDIOS IN THE SIXTIES.

Early Years

I have no idea why my mother took me as an eight-year-old to join the parish church choir. My father was an atheist, and she drifted in and out of Christianity throughout her life, never attending church on anything like a regular basis until my father retired many years later. Perhaps it was because I had shown an interest in it at school, although my only memory of singing in the choir at my primary school was, when I was five, being pulled out of line and slapped on the calf by an extremely rotund Miss Butterworth for talking when I should have been listening. I remember this incident clearly and have often wondered why, as I can recall very little else from those early years. Maybe it was the vicious expression on her fat face. I remember she bit her bottom lip as she applied her hand to my bare leg with as much force as she could muster. I was embarrassed and cried and could not understand the satisfaction she seemed to get from the experience.

There I was, committed to two choir practices a week, on Tuesdays and Fridays, three services on Sunday, and as many weddings on a Saturday that required the services of the boy sopranos. Weddings were the best because we got paid for them. At first, I got nine pence for each one, which increased to one shilling and sixpence when I eventually became head chorister. So if we did three or four weddings on a Saturday the proceeds would go a long way in Lowman's store, with a lot left over for the odd puncture kit for the bike or a visit to the local indoor swimming pool. Four Old English pennies to get in and three to buy a bag of hot chips from the fish and chip shop on the way home.

My life very quickly began to revolve around the church and the two-and-a-half-mile walk to and from it. It would take me past Lowman's and on to the churchyard with its narrow, winding asphalt path that threaded its way through tilting ancient gravestones leading straight past the vestry to the west door of the church. The path was faintly lit with sparsely placed lampposts, which on a foggy night in midwinter threw a mysterious damp haze on the gravestones and the gathering of young boys waiting impatiently for the arrival of our great leader, Mr. Felton Rapley, the choirmaster and extremely accomplished organist of St. Martin's Parish Church in Epsom.

Mr. Rapley was a very large man who always seemed to be in a hurry. He had a serious, all-knowing face like an owl. He had thick horn-rim glasses, thinning gray hair, and a gray walrus mustache. He was intimidating to an eight-year-old. However, he was to become my mentor during the next few years. Perhaps he was my first hero.

Sometimes I would arrive early for choir practice, and as I approached the church, I could hear him rehearsing his next recital. I would sit outside on the wall by the vestry door in the dark, transfixed by the sheer size of the organ's sound penetrating the dimly lit stained-glass windows. The whole sensation was magnified by the fact that it was taking place in the middle of a graveyard that dated back to the fifteenth century.

There is nothing quite like the experience of singing with a large group of people, your senses being bombarded by all those harmonics and actually contributing some of your own. Felton Rapley spotted my enthusiasm quite early on and quietly took me under his wing. As I grew older he encouraged me more and more, giving me the odd solo and slowly boosting my confidence until he made me head chorister at the age of eleven.

He was considered to be one of the finest pipe organists in the country, performing regularly on BBC radio. He would give a recital every fourth Sunday after Evensong, and one such Sunday he asked if I would stay after the service and turn pages for him. I naturally jumped at the chance to see the great man perform. We could never see him when he played during a service. The organ loft was way up above us some thirty or forty feet, surrounded by this massive array of pipes, rather like a giant Gulliver's panpipes. Although this was opposite where I stood in the choir stalls, I could only ever see his balding head and his shoulders swaying, physically accenting what he played. He had a long mirror up above his head so he could keep his eye on the transgressors eating boiled sweets or reading the *Beano* or *Eagle* comic during one of those interminably boring sermons.

Evensong finished and I followed Mr. Rapley as he propelled himself up the steep narrow stone spiral staircase that led from the vestry up to the organ loft. His enormous frame brushing the walls on either side, with his long black gown flowing behind him. He always seemed short of breath on the flat, as a result of him smoking large numbers of Senior Service cigarettes when outside the confines of the church, so by the time he made it to the top he seemed to be completely knackered. He sat down heavily on one end of the organ bench, bent over, and with some difficulty changed his shoes for a pair of patent leather slippers. I remember being terribly impressed, having never seen anything quite so opulent. He swung round, squeezing himself between the bench and the three keyboards that fanned out in front of him, set the music on its stand, and pressed a couple of preset buttons, which caused the two vertical banks of porcelain knobs on either side of the keyboard to jump in and out with great speed and a resounding thump. As he began to play, he was transformed before my very eyes. His energy level seemed to quadruple. The cumbersome movement of his somewhat overweight body disappeared and became fluid, his fingers flying across the keyboard with extraordinary speed and accuracy. His shiny feet dancing over the pedals with the dexterity of a ballet dancer.

I found this transformation, and the sound that was belting out of the organ pipes, completely enthralling. The sheer energy and emotion of it had a profound impact on me, as I realized that the performance of a piece of music could have such a dramatic effect not only on the listener but also on the performer.

Most years when we were children, my mother would take my two older sisters, my younger brother, and me to stay with her brother Robert, known as Chum, on his farm in Devon for our summer holidays. It was an idyllic, magical place for me. Beautiful rolling countryside, woodland, and streams to explore. All new experiences to interest and excite the senses of a small child from just outside the suburbs of London.

My uncle Chum quickly became one of my favorite people. He was an extremely handsome man with a kind, somewhat weathered face and a wonderful twinkle in his eye. He would sit and tell stories of his life before the Second World War. How he would race his Bugatti at Brooklands motor racing track in the thirties. My mother had newspaper clippings of him and his older brother George, who raced for the Bentley team and had won the European Grand Prix in the thirties.

It was in that farmhouse kitchen that I became totally infatuated by a completely different form of music than that of the church choir. In the evening, after dinner, he would play Django Reinhardt records and then take out this old acoustic guitar and sing these wonderful American folk songs. My uncle was a fine player and had the most encapsulating voice, but more than anything it was his personality and the manner in which he performed the songs that made such an enormous impression on me, as he turned into the character that each song's story required with consummate ease. It was a similar experience to that of watching Felton Rapley play the organ, the performer being transformed into someone else as the music took over.

When I was twelve or thirteen, the local operatic society performed Handel's *Messiah* at the church and I was asked to be a soloist. Being the only child, and I am sure for dramatic effect, I sang my solo from the sanctity of the organ loft with the comfort of being close to Mr. Rapley. This was much better, as I was looking down at the scene from on high and felt secure from the massed singers and audience of several hundred people below. Shortly after this, Mr. Rapley suggested that I audition for a weekly religious program on BBC radio that featured a boy soprano. The lad who had the job was getting on in years and his voice was about to break. I passed the audition and excitedly waited for my big opportunity, that is, until my voice broke, and that was the end of that. The first of many disappointments in the music business.

. . .

I called into Mr. Lowman's store on the way back from church one Sunday and we got chatting. I told him how my next-door neighbor had lent me a four-string tenor guitar and how I was trying to teach myself to play it. He asked me to wait a minute and reappeared with a pristine, lime-green Guild electric guitar. "Borrow this," he said. "I'm looking after it for my brother." I had never seen anything like it. I took it home and just looked at it in the case for several days, petrified that some harm would come to it if I took it out. I eventually plucked up the courage and as I had no idea how to play it, sat around posing with it in my bedroom, periodically checking myself in the mirror. I soon returned it to Mr. Lowman with much gratitude. I was hooked.

I stayed on at the church as a server and started going to the church youth club on Wednesday nights. Among other delights, we would have discussion nights and play table tennis and were taught ballroom dancing, which didn't appeal to me at all, but at least you got to put your arm around a girl legitimately. One evening we had a talent night. I remember a boy in his early teens no one had seen before, who sat with his legs swinging over the front edge of the stage and played an acoustic guitar. He was pretty good, he may have even won, but I don't think anyone in the hall that night had any idea that he was to become such an innovative force in modern music. This was to be my first meeting with Jimmy Page.

By the time I was fifteen, in 1957, my head was being turned by traditional jazz. There was a band that had been formed by some of the seniors at school, but when I showed interest, I was rejected on sight, with a cuff round the ear for impertinence, as I was considered to be nothing but a "snotty" youngster from the middle school. The clarinet player in the band was Dick Morrissey, who went on to become one of the all-time great English modern jazz saxophonists. Many years later, I booked him as a soloist on a couple of sessions at Olympic Studios. When I reminded him of the incident at school, he was kind enough to say he remembered it but I'm pretty sure he didn't.

So, not to be put off, I made myself a tea chest bass and started playing with the Terry Emptage Band at my older sister Sue's college's student union Thursday-night do. I was several years younger than the rest of the band so there was not a great deal of communication between us but I didn't care. I was playing and having a ball.

It is the simplest of instruments to make and to play. Having acquired from the local grocer a large square plywood crate, originally used for shipping loose tea, you turn it upside down (as the top has been removed to get at the tea), and nail a long pole to the middle of one side. Then attach one end of a piece of picture-hanging cord to the top of the pole and the other through a hole in the middle of the top of the chest. To play it, you just put one foot on the box and vigorously attack the cord with your right hand in some sort of rhythm while altering the pitch by pulling back and releasing the pole with your left.

My biggest problem was getting around. I managed to devise a way of carrying the bass on my bicycle. I would put it over my shoulder and stuff the pole under the handlebars and pedal for miles in a most precarious manner. Everything would be fine if it was not a windy evening. It's a wonder I ever made it anywhere unscathed, or unarrested for that matter, for being a danger to others on the road.

Soon there were more gigs around the area. I couldn't travel much more than ten miles if I was to be fit enough to play on arrival. This included a regular Wednesday-night gig at the Organ Inn, a local jazz pub, where I was used only if the real bass player couldn't make it, but I didn't care, this was the big time.

My sister Sue had a portable record player and, being three years older than me, found me to be nothing more than an annoyance throughout our youth. Therefore the record player was strictly off-limits, with very rare exceptions. I remember she bought a 78 of "Little Rock Getaway" by Les Paul and Mary Ford. It was a completely new sound. Les Paul was the first artist to use multitracking. He would record a guitar part on a mono machine, then play it back and record it onto another machine while adding a second guitar, repeating the process until he had the arrangement he wanted. Then he would do the same with Mary Ford's voice, adding her three or four times in harmony with herself. This was some years before the advent of multitrack recording as we know it today. Along with every other punter, I knew nothing of this and just thought it was a great sound. His innovative approach to recording led to the formation of the Ampex company, who produced the first multitrack tape machines with Les being given the second one off the line.

Les Paul's records almost paled into insignificance when I heard "Rock Island Line" by Lonnie Donegan for the first time on the radio. I had heard nothing like it and rushed out and bought it the next day. This was the first record I ever owned, and it and the 10-inch album Donegan released shortly thereafter became my staple diet for the next few months. He started the skiffle craze, which led to a fairly short-lived dominance of the charts by several other bands that copied him, and led me to American folk music and on to the blues.

. . .

In the summer, I took a job on a farm to earn the money for my first guitar. Having slaved and sneezed (from hay fever) my way through eight weeks of milling and shoveling feed and the foulest-smelling pig shit at three pounds ten shillings a week, I finally had the twenty-seven quid required. I rode home on my bike from my last day's work only to find my pay packet for the previous two weeks had fallen out of my pocket. Fortunately my eldest sister, Dilys, bless her heart, learned of my predicament, came to my rescue, and gave me the balance.

Peter Sandford, a man who lived a few houses up the road from my parents, heard that I had bought the guitar and encouraged my interest by showing me his incredible collection of books and records on folk and blues. He was extremely kind to me, lending me anything I wanted to absorb in my own time. He introduced me to Snooks Eaglin, Brownie McGhee and Sonny Terry, Woody Guthrie, and Burl Ives. I would take records and songbooks home to my room and learn them, playing them over and over again in the dark so that I could not cheat and look where my fingers were going on the neck of the guitar.

I started to meet a few friends in a park on the way home from our respective schools. We would chat about the latest Elvis or Fats Domino records and soon began to meet at each other's houses, parents permitting, to play music and dance. I was not that comfortable dancing, which I am sure, on reflection, was one of my main motivations to get involved with helping to provide the music to dance to. The crowd of kids got bigger and bigger, and we started to meet in the park at weekends. The great thing about "The Gang," as it quickly became known, was that it seemed completely classless. Pretty soon there were thirty or forty of us, sons and daughters from all walks of life, meeting as frequently as possible. There was nothing territorial or aggressive about it and could not be likened in any way to the modern gangs of today.

The boys would turn up on their track bikes, the girls on their horses or on foot, and the usual teenage exchange would take place. Girls preening, boys showing off to the girls and each other. Sometimes I would take my guitar, and pretty soon my friend Rob Mayhew brought his. He was far more accomplished than I and helped me onto the bottom rung as a musician, from which, I might add, I never ascended. We started singing together, mostly Buddy Holly and Everly Brothers stuff.

One day, my next-door neighbor Hugh Oliver, who was at least fifteen years older than me, called me from over the fence between our two properties and handed me the most wonderful, satirical lyrics he had written, and asked if I would be interested in putting them to music. The results of which Rob and I would try out on this motley bunch of teenagers with varying degrees of success.

Sometimes smaller groups of us would meet in the Harlequin coffee bar in Cheam, making a round of toast and a cup of tea last until we were asked to leave by the owner, Mrs. Hughes. Little did I know then that twenty years later she would become my mother-in-law.

It was through the window of the Harlequin that I was to catch my first sight of Ian Stewart. He would ride by on his racing bike, cutting a very athletic figure in his leather cycling shorts, his exaggerated chin thrust forward from the exertion of pedaling up the hill in Cheam High Street. He was three or four years older than me and we were not to meet until I was seventeen or eighteen, and boy did that change my life.

The bicycles gave way to motorbikes, the girls' waists seemed to get smaller as their skirts got fuller. Then along came Pat. The first American I ever met. He had a new 650cc Norton and wore white T-shirts and jeans. A regular bloody James Dean. Much cooler than any of us. Enough to make you puke. All the girls thought he was great looking and swooned all over him, but for me he had one saving grace: Jimmy Reed records. This was yet another new sound that completely blew me away. To be fair, Pat turned out to be a really nice guy. Fortunately for the rest of the boys, he was around for only one summer.

I left school in July of 1959, at the age of seventeen, not knowing what to do. I only knew that I didn't want to work in an office or in any nine-to-five job. Agriculture interested me, but without substantial capital it seemed pointless to pursue as a career. It was about this time that two of my best pals, Rob Mayhew and Colin Golding, and I decided to form a group that I managed and was the sometime singer with, called The Presidents. Well, it wasn't exactly a group, more a random collection of guys playing things. It evolved out of the Gang and its insatiable need for cheap entertainment. We started out playing for our own amusement at each other's parties. In its final configuration, without me singing, it became a really good cover band. We would rehearse each week, and I realize now that the experience of listening to and dissecting the popular records of the day in order to replicate them accurately with the band was excellent subliminal training for my future as an engineer and producer.

As the band became more popular, we decided to find a regular venue to play. We took a room at the back of the Red Lion pub in Sutton every other Friday. It was an instant success, and after paying the rent we would make £30 or £40 a night. Which in those days was a fortune.

I had been working in a department store on Saturdays for the previous year, so I took a full-time job there until my exam results came through and I could decide what to do. The results proved to be even worse than expected. I had taken eight subjects and passed only two, history and English literature. This came as a great disappointment to my parents, and gloom set in as they wondered what would become of me without the required academic qualifications for further education and therefore entry into any of the more recognized professions.

Out of the blue, my sister Sue came home from work one day and asked me if I would be interested in the idea of working at a recording studio. Her boss had a girlfriend, and while she was waiting in the outer office for him, Sue mentioned to her that she had a brother whose main interest in life was music. She responded by telling Sue that she owned a small record label that specialized in Welsh music and would try to get me an interview at the recording studio she used—that is, if I was interested. Needless to say, it had never entered my mind to work in the music business. I knew absolutely nothing about recording and had never thought about or known anyone working anywhere but in the usual and more mundane professions. So this opportunity came about only as a result of a polite conversation between two women who did not even know each other. I have often thought what an extraordinary turn of fate this was.

It was with great apprehension that I went for the interview a few days later. The studio turned out to be IBC in Portland Place, which was without a doubt the finest independent recording studio in Europe at that time. The manager, a seemingly pleasant Welshman named Alan Stagg, asked me a bunch of technical questions about recording, none of which I could answer. He said there was nothing available right then but the next time there was a vacancy he would certainly consider me for a job. The only thing that seemed to be in my favor, as I pondered the experience on the train back to Epsom, was the fact that I had a Welsh grandfather, a Welsh name, and that I'd had some formal training in a choir. God bless the Red Dragon!

I returned to my job at the store thinking I would probably never hear from the studio again. This would almost certainly be true if I had been left to my own devices. About six weeks had passed since the interview when my mother suggested to me that, as I had heard nothing, I should call Mr. Stagg and jog his memory. I argued, saying that, after all, the man had said that he would consider me at the next opportunity. Fortunately my mother insisted on my making the call, pointing out that I had nothing to lose. So I rang Alan Stagg, and having reminded him who I was, he said that one of the senior engineers at the studio had handed in his notice that day and that this would create a vacancy at the bottom of the ladder for a trainee, so when could I start? I am convinced that if I had not called that day I would never have heard from IBC again and would probably have not got involved in music as a career at all.

I started work at IBC the very next day, as a lowly assistant engineer. This meant setting up the studio before each session to the engineer's requirements, keeping continuity, and taking the blame for anything that did not work, while receiving varying amounts of verbal abuse from my superiors before, during, and after the session, and then stripping the studio afterward, with a great deal of tea making and equipment polishing thrown in.

The first session I was assigned was for Lonnie Donegan. This was too good to be true. He was still my favorite recording artist. I even discovered that the picture on the front cover of my much-coveted 10-inch album was taken in studio B at IBC. It was all too much for a young boy.

IBC had no affiliation with any one label, being privately owned. In those days, RCA, Decca, Pye, and EMI all had their own studios, leaving the rest for the independents. As a result we had an incredible variety of artists, musicians, and clients passing through. The music ranged from the most idiotic jingles to big bands—from Julian Bream to Alma Cogan, the music for the CBS TV series *Wagon Train* to a modern jazz quintet, and the odd excursion out to record a symphony orchestra or pop concert in far-flung venues.

As my feet touched the ground again after the initial shock of getting the job, I realized that my primary objective at IBC should be that it would give me the opportunity to get my foot in the door and explore the music business with the view of being discovered as a singer. Although fascinated by the recording process, I was far more interested in music and those who made it. I quickly realized that the best thing to do was to work as efficiently as possible while keeping my head down, observing as much as I could to establish who did what, when, where, why, and to whom.

In those days, record producers were called A&R men, meaning "artists and repertoire." They all worked for a label and were responsible for the artists they were assigned or they brought to the label and for the repertoire of music those artists recorded. Very few singers wrote their own material, so the A&R men would select songs from the vast array that was pitched to them by the music publishers. This made them extremely powerful, with the potential to manipulate the situation to their own benefit. For example, they might have their own publishing company and increase their earning capacity by doing deals with other publishers to split the publishing of a song, or perhaps take the publishing of a B-side or album track in exchange for agreeing to record a song with a successful artist.

The A&R man would pick the song and, having routined it with the artist and chosen the correct key to perform it in, would decide on the arranger, who in turn would use a fixer to book the musicians. This would invariably be an older musician who acted as an agent and union representative for session musicians he booked. Sometimes the A&R man would be involved in the details of the arrangement and of the choice of musicians, sometimes not. Most A&R men had a favorite recording engineer they worked with and would very often choose a studio based on who worked there, as there were no freelance engineers then. All of this would be done within the restrictions of a budget, which the A&R man would draw up and have approved by his superior in the company and thereafter be responsible for. He would then supervise the session, making sure that the engineer, arranger, musicians, and artist performed to his satisfaction. Hopefully making the song sound as he had envisaged. So it became apparent fairly quickly how important the engineer was to the success of a studio, both in personality and variety of musical taste as well as the more obvious technical and creative abilities.

IBC was not only the best-equipped independent studio in Europe but it was also blessed with a great assortment of engineering talent, starting with Eric Tomlinson, who was the senior engineer on the staff when I began and, in my opinion, was one of the finest in the world. I remember that he had this habit of standing with one foot on top of the other while he worked, his hands flying around the console, never needing more than one run-through of the most complex of orchestral pieces before having it memorized, balanced, and ready to record. He was extremely kind to me, and I learned a great deal from watching the master at work.

Then there was the very aptly named Ray Prickett. Although he suffered from little or no sense of humor and treated me like an unpleasant smell, he was still a great engineer. Among many others, he engineered most of the records that Alan Freeman produced for Pye Records. Petula Clark, Lonnie Donegan, and Kenny Ball being a few of the many successes he had.

John Timperley, who was a little older than me, was another who developed his own approach to recording with great success and went on to have his own studio in London.

Alan Stagg was also an engineer, specializing in classical recording. IBC being the only independent studio in Europe that had its own mobile recording unit meant we could go to any of the bigger venues required for recording large orchestras and choirs. Alan did very little recording, which turned out to be a good thing, as it quickly became apparent to me that he was not much of a specialist. However, he made sure the studio was always the first with the latest equipment, and the fact that it had such a great variety of talented engineers must have, to a large extent, been down to him.

Some of the classical sessions were engineered by David Price, an unpleasant little shit of a man, as I remember. He had a client, a BBC radio producer in real life moonlighting as a classical record producer. He bordered on certifiable, and like so many producers was an egomaniac. Most of the classical stuff was done on location, in large halls in London that could accommodate a symphony orchestra, like Wandsworth, Hammersmith, or Walthamstow town hall.

Today, mobile recording units are purpose-built trucks. Back then, the equipment was loose in boxes. We would hire a furniture-removal van, load it up, then unload at the venue, where we would be allocated a room to use as a control room. This invariably would be a dressing room, chosen by some faceless individual who clearly didn't want you there, based on the fact that the room was up several flights of stairs and as far away from the auditorium as possible. Having assembled the equipment in the control room, the engineer and his assistant would leave the tech to make sure that it worked and was aligned properly, while they ran the miles of cable to the auditorium, put up the microphones, and arranged the setup of the orchestra in the space available to them in the hall. All this to say that, by the time people started to arrive at the session for a ten-o'clock start, you had already done a full day's work and were completely knackered.

This producer would arrive in the nick of time, throw down his briefcase containing the score, walk over to the loudspeakers, demand that they be turned flat out, and stick his ear right inside them. If he could detect the slightest hum or buzz, all hell would break loose.

I remember one such occasion: fourteen strings and a harpsichord at Red Lion Square in London. Not the most scintillating session I had ever been assigned to. The producer had thrown his usual wobbly, and David Price had blamed the poor unsuspecting tech. I had worked late the night before and, having had only two or three hours' sleep, made the mistake of nodding off during a take, only to be awakened by a swift belt round the ear from David Price, with the producer doubtless applauding in the corner. Looking back, it is extraordinary what people got away with in those days. However, I never fell asleep during a session again.

The other major difference in the early days was that the maintenance department would be much larger and play a key role in the development of the studio, designing and building the consoles that we used in-house. This becoming a most important part of a studio's reputation for being up-to-date with the latest technology. Nowadays it is equally important to stay abreast of the times; however, this is not achieved with the individuality that existed in the sixties, as nearly all recording equipment is now mass-produced and name-branded.

The late great Joe Meek used IBC on occasion. He had his own studio at home, where he developed his extraordinary sound, but he would often bring his tapes in to run them through one of our home-built equalizers to cheer them up a bit. I think he was frowned on by the powers that be, and as I was the most junior in the place I would be given the job of looking after him. What a great opportunity for me. He was a great and innovative engineer and a quiet, kind, and seemingly egoless man.

Last but not least was Terry Johnson. He left school illegally at fifteen and lied about his age to get the job at IBC. By the time I arrived he was already doing sessions as an engineer at sixteen. To say he was a natural is something of an understatement. He was an extraordinary talent. For eighteen months or so we were pretty much inseparable. We soon discovered that we shared the same taste in music and sound and became close friends, closing ranks against the somewhat disapproving attitude of the senior engineers at IBC.

As that first year progressed, music began to change and the demand increased for English records to sound more and more like what was going on in America. Most of the older engineers didn't get it and were entirely dismissive. This meant that Terry, being as young as he was and having a natural enthusiasm for trying new ideas, was in great demand, and he pulled me along with him.

We were constantly being challenged on how to re-create sounds that were coming from America. This proved particularly difficult because American musicians were creating a very different sound and feel to the English guys, something I was to have illustrated in triplicate when we had the privilege of prerecording the music for a TV show with Dusty Springfield called *The Sounds of Motown*. They flew the band in from Motown and set up straight off the plane. We turned the mics on and instantly there it was. Just like the records we had been listening to. I remember Terry and me looking at each

AT IBC IN THE EARLY SIXTIES, OBVIOUSLY EXTREMELY
PISSED OFF ABOUT SOMETHING.

other with great relief, as we had imagined that we were in for a struggle, not knowing how the hell that sound was achieved.

We had to figure out new methods of recording to capture and do justice to the new, louder rock and roll as it took over. Previously, the loudest sound anyone had recorded was the cannon in the 1812 Overture.

The studio was a constant buzz of activity. In a normal day, both studios A and B would have three sessions, very often each having a different client, musicians, and artist. The whole approach to recording was so different then. Even the dress code: a jacket, collar, and tie for all engineers and assistants. White coats, collars, and ties for the technical department. Sessions lasted three hours when as many as four songs would be cut. So albums were very often cut in a day. The volume and variety of work was fantastic, the building being constantly flooded and drained of an extraordinary assortment of people, from the most colorful, extrovert artist to the most bland suburban string player, hurrying off to his next seven pounds ten shillings, wondering what was going to win the 2:30 at Sandown Park.

In the late fifties and early sixties almost everything was recorded in mono, as very few people had the facility to play stereo. The exception was the odd classical recording. Unlike today, it was all recorded at once, so when the three-hour session was finished, the tape could go straight to a cutting room to transfer the sound to disc and then on to the factory to be processed and pressed onto vinyl. If it was a single, and therefore did not require a sleeve with artwork, it could be in the shops in a few days. In fact, very few artists got to make an album in those days, as you had to have a few hits under your belt before it was justified. Then you were allowed to make an EP, finally graduating to ten or twelve cuts on an LP.

Jack Good

The first real extrovert I met was Jack Good. He was the complete antithesis of what you would expect a rock and roll producer to be. Immaculate in Savile Row suits, with an Oxford accent and a chubby, somewhat impish face rounded off with large horn-rim glasses. His only concession to nonconformity in his dress being Cuban-heeled Beatle boots. In fact, he was the first person I ever saw wearing them. He was charming, hysterically funny, and without ego. He was a breath of fresh air for Terry Johnson and me when we were given him as a client, as most of the other producers we were required to work with were far too full of their own self-importance.

Jack started rock and roll TV in England, producing a weekly show for the BBC called *Six-Five Special* that very quickly became an absolute must for most teenagers in the UK. He went on to have the same success for ITV with *Oh Boy!*, which is where Terry and I came in. IBC was booked to prerecord the music every Thursday of the show's run and we were given the job.

It was mayhem. Although they only booked one studio, the entire building would be taken over for the day by the English rock and roll elite of the day: Joe Brown, Marty Wilde, Billy Fury, Wee Willie Harris, to name but a few. They were accompanied by a staff band, which in turn were supplemented by the Vernons Girls, an all-glamour group of young girls who sang and danced on the show. There was a narrow staircase running up the center of the building, which became the place for the artists to hang out while waiting for their call. This soon became known as "Chat-Up Alley." God knows what went on out there while we were working. I do know that Joe and Marty eventually married two of the girls.

All of this was controlled perfectly by Jack, who came from another planet to this unruly lot of state school dropouts. They all loved him, not only for his personality but because they shared his great passion for American rock and roll.

Jack started to produce records, with great success. He did most of his recording with Terry and me at IBC. Then he was asked to do a special with The Beatles for Granada TV called *Around The Beatles*. He brought P. J. Proby to England from America to appear on the show and made him a star. Proby's only claim to fame at that time was that he could imitate pretty much anyone. He would get calls from publishers to cut demos of songs they were trying to pitch to Elvis or Roy Orbison. I remember him telling me that he had spent so much time imitating other singers that he no longer knew which was his real voice.

This was my first experience of The Beatles. I say "experience" as I did not really meet them, being only the second engineer on the session. We cut instrumental tracks with them to sing live to on the show. TV sound was pretty awful in those days and no one in their right mind would play live. Apart from the fact that recording technology has changed so much since then, none of the TV sound engineers or set designers had a clue about this new loud music. The sets were created for visual effect and not acoustically designed to cope.

The one thing that struck me about this session was how relatively ordinary they sounded without the vocals. They could have been any competent group of the day, but as soon as the voices were added the magic was there. It has always amazed me how they progressed as writers, musicians, and producers from this already exalted position.

Sunday Sessions

Weekends were almost never booked in those first two years I was at IBC. So we were allowed to use the studio on Sundays to record our own projects. It all started with me and my friend Rob Mayhew recording a few demos, with John Timperley or Terry Johnson engineering. It was with one of these recordings that I attempted to be "discovered" as a vocalist, with a song I had written with my neighbor Hugh Oliver, called "Sioux Indian."

I set a trap for Jack Good. I waited until I heard him coming up the stairs to go into studio A's control room for the start of a session and having left the door wide open, started to play my tape in the dubbing room next door. It worked. He stuck his head in and said, "Who's that? It sounds really good." Within a few weeks he had convinced Dick Rowe, then head of A&R at Decca Records, to sign me to my first recording contract, and Jack had produced my first single.

He used the hot rhythm section of the day: Andy White, drums; Big Jim Sullivan, guitar; Andy Whale, bass; and Reg Guest, piano. My mate Terry engineered. The whole experience was surreal, as I knew everyone so well and previously they had only known me as an engineer on the other side of the glass. The record did not make much of a dent, so my singing career was put on hold for a while, but it did mean that The Presidents could put "Featuring Decca Recording Star Glyn Johns" on their posters.

Soon I realized that I could use the time to experiment and get some experience at the console, and I put the word out that you could get free studio time at my Sunday sessions. This attracted a crowd of exciting young musicians. Among them was Jimmy Page, who my pal Colin Golding had told me about. They were both at Kingston Art School—not far from where we all lived—along with Eric Clapton.

I suggested that I might be able to get Jimmy some paying sessions, but initially he declined, saying he would lose his grant at school if it became known that he had an income. It was not long before he changed his mind, and in a short space of time he had replaced Big Jim Sullivan as the number-one session guitarist in London.

Cyril Davies turned up one Sunday, a wonderful harmonica player and vocalist who was one of the founders of the rhythm and blues movement in Britain along with Ian Stewart, Alexis Korner, and Brian Jones. He brought Nicky Hopkins with him to play. I went to set up the mics on the piano and was greeted by a softly spoken, extremely gaunt young man with a gray pallor and clothes that were several sizes too big. His whole demeanor was devoid of energy. However, when the session started, his playing was the most fluid, melodic, and technically perfect that I had ever heard. All achieved with a minimum of movement and an unchanging facial expression. I asked him at the end of the day why I had not come across him before and if he would allow me to recommend him for sessions in the future.

We were to become great friends. Over the ensuing years, I got him sessions with The Who, The Kinks, and eventually the Stones, where he was a tremendous influence, playing on the songs that Ian Stewart had refused because they were not the blues. I think the era that he and Mick Taylor were in the band resulted in the best records they made.

Later, in 1969, on a Stones session for *Let It Bleed*, Keith didn't show. So while we were waiting, Nicky started jamming on the piano with Charlie and Bill. Pretty soon Mick got a harmonica and was soon joined by Ry Cooder, who was sitting in with the band that night. Jack Nitzsche had brought him over from California to play on the soundtrack to the movie *Performance* that we had finished a couple of days earlier. I ran the tape machine and the result was an album called *Jamming with Edward*, eventually released on Rolling Stones Records in 1972. It is just a bit of fun, showing Nicky's sense of humor and extraordinary technique, and it is great to hear Ry playing with Bill and Charlie. Definitely worth a listen.

Andrew Oldham appeared one Sunday. Dressed in a cloak and carrying a silver-topped cane. Which is the only reason I remember him, as he is not a musician and could only have come as a guest of one of the guys on the session. I think he was starting out in PR and, having got Brian Epstein on his books, was obviously sniffing around the music business either for clients or to check out a new career. He was to become one of the most influential individuals in the industry in the sixties, managing The Rolling Stones and starting one of the first independent labels in the UK, Immediate Records.

First Session,
1960

In 1960 I got my first opportunity to actually sit at the console as the engineer. I was the assistant on the recording of a Son et Lumière production about the Battle of Trafalgar staged on Lord Nelson's ship the *Victory* in Portsmouth Harbour. Lord Nelson was played by Sir Laurence Olivier, who wanted to work on a Saturday, and the engineer, Ray Prickett, refused to work on weekends, so I was given the job. I was petrified. Fortunately, the director, Peter Wood, was a charming and kind man and did his best to put me at ease, knowing that this was my first session in charge. Just the idea of being in the presence of the great man was bad enough. It only involved one microphone, so not a lot could go wrong. Pathetic really.

Unfortunately, the news of Olivier's intention to divorce Vivien Leigh and marry Joan Plowright had broken in the press that morning. So when he burst out of the elevator on the third floor and into studio B with a flurry of agitated entourage, there was steam coming out of every orifice.

After a few minutes' conversation with Peter Wood in private, he had calmed down and we were ready to start work. I had prepared a table with a green baize cloth, a decanter of water and a glass, and a chair that I had stolen from the studio owner's office. No tubular metal and canvas musician's chair for God.

He was to read the most important and emotive speech in the whole piece—Nelson's letter to Lady Hamilton the night before he died at the Battle of Trafalgar. His transformation into character was extraordinary to watch. Those of us present being stunned into silence by the end of the one and only take.

Later that morning he was joined by a group of young actors who had to play a scene with him. It was quite obvious from the start that they were all in awe of him, but within minutes he had them completely at ease in his presence. A true professional. His personal problems left at the door, his concern for others and the job at hand taking precedence.

The thrill of working at IBC was the variety. You never quite knew what would come through the door next. From a jingle for soap powder in the morning to a traditional jazz band in the afternoon to a thirty-piece orchestra with a pop star of the day in the evening. Followed the next day by the London Symphony Orchestra with a sixty-piece choir at one of London's town halls. Some of it was inordinately boring but it was all a great experience. I was not just learning about the technical aspects of recording but witnessing the way people behaved and manipulated one another in a creative environment.

My first music session as the engineer was with Joe Brown. A kinder man I have yet to meet. He was a big star, and quite rightly so, and was to record a follow-up to his latest hit. His A&R man at Pye Records was Tony Hatch, another unpleasant man with a massive ego. Unbelievably full of his own self-importance, with all the charm of a 1950s block of council flats. Up until that evening he had barely acknowledged my existence as an assistant to the engineer on many of his sessions.

It was to be a twenty-eight-piece orchestra with Joe singing live. Two songs, an A- and a B-side for a single, to be recorded in mono in a three-hour session. So, no tinkering with it afterward. The engineer I was supposed to be assisting had been taken ill earlier in the day and, as no one else was available, I was once again up by default.

Hatch arrived and did nothing to calm my nerves by throwing a massive wobbly and declaring that it was too late to cancel the session, which is what he would have preferred to do, as I was not competent in his eyes.

The session went really well. Joe was lovely and seemed very pleased with the result. The following morning I was summoned to Alan Stagg's office and informed that there was to be an inquiry into the previous night's session. Tony Hatch had called and told him that it had been a disaster as a result of my inexperience and that Pye Records would hold IBC responsible for the entire cost of the session. An inquest was held and the master tape critiqued, with IBC taking the view that there was nothing wrong with the recording, and Tony Hatch was told to take a flying leap. Pye Records was one of the studio's biggest clients, so this was quite a brave move on Alan Stagg's part, as he could easily have lost their business. I don't remember the title but I am pretty sure that the record was released and was successful for Joe. So the good guys won all round, and I was off and running, having survived what seemed at the time to be "trial by fire."

Singer-Songwriter/
Freelance Producer,
Early Sixties

I n the early sixties, the record business underwent a massive change as the singer-songwriter emerged on the scene, The Beatles and Bob Dylan leading the way. It was not too long before everyone had to write their own material in order to be original. It was no longer enough just to be a good singer and performer.

It was at this point that the independent producer came into being. Previously, the A&R man had always been an employee of the record company, and having signed the act and found the material, he then produced the record. As the singer-songwriter appeared, the A&R man took on the responsibility of finding and signing the talent to the label and supervising the recording career of the artist, delegating the making of the record, and very often the selection of material on it, to an independent producer. Clearly this expanded the creative options available to record companies, and although it was standard practice for independent producers' contracts to be exclusive for a period of three to five years, it was not too long until artists and labels were allowed to change producers at will.

Mike Smith was the first example of an independent producer that I can recall. He worked as an A&R man at Decca, where he had a string of hits with such artists as Brian Poole and the Tremeloes and Dave Berry. I can only guess that he was approached by other labels to work for them and realized the potential of becoming an independent producer as a result. He was a great guy, and it must have taken enormous courage to step out and break the mold.

It is interesting to note that the old-time songwriter very rarely even made the demo of the song he or she had just written. It was common practice to hire a professional demo singer to present the song on tape from which acetates would be cut, and they would be carted around to the A&R men and sometimes directly to the artist, by the song pluggers who worked for the publishers and whose sole job was to pitch the song and get it recorded. So it would seem that the art of songwriting was singularly that, and rarely had anything to do with an unusually high ability to either sing or play, until the new breed came along.

Stu '62

In 1962, Colin Golding, the bass player in The Presidents, introduced me to Ian Stewart, or "Stu" as he was affectionately known. Colin told me that he knew this guy who lived locally who had a vast collection of jazz and blues records. So he was definitely to be checked out. The friendship that grew from that meeting had an immense effect on my life. We met and discussed our mutual interest in the blues. He was so modest that it wasn't for some time that I found out that he played the piano and that he and a bunch of like-minded blues enthusiasts had put a band together called The Rolling Stones. In fact, he was responsible for starting the band with Brian Jones, having answered an advertisement Brian had placed in *Jazz News* earlier that year.

So it was through him that I was to become involved with the Stones from the very beginning through the first thirteen years of their career.

In late 1964 my father retired and my parents moved to Gloucestershire, so I had to find a place to live. I was twenty-two years old and should have left home long before. The house that I wanted to rent was in my hometown of Epsom. It was twelve guineas a week, an amount I could not afford on my own, so I had to think of someone to share with. The idea did not appeal to me at all. The only person I knew that I would even consider was Stu. He was living very comfortably with his parents. Meals cooked, laundry done, et cetera. So when I called to ask him to join me, his initial reaction was a flat no. It was only when I pointed out the benefit of having the freedom to bring girls home that he changed his mind. However, this was only on the condition that he would have nothing to do with the upkeep of the garden, and under no circumstances would he ever do any cleaning in the house. To say that domesticity was not Stu's forte is something of an understatement.

We moved in together and the one piece of furniture that Stu brought with him was his upright piano. I remember waking up one morning to the sound of the most extraordinary blues music wafting up from the living room along with the usual smell of deliberately burned toast that he would make every morning. I went to investigate, to find Stu sitting at the piano, wearing nothing but his underpants, with an open letter on the stool beside him. The contents of the letter, apparently from an old flame, had upset him to such an extent that the only way he could deal with it was to play the blues. I felt like I was intruding, so I went back to my room where, for the next hour or so, I was treated to this impromptu outpouring of emotion by one of the finest blues musicians I have ever come across.

There were three bedrooms in the house, so he suggested that we invite a pal of his, Brian "Knocker" Wiles, to join us to share the rent.

The arrangement worked quite well, as we saw very little of each other. Brian had a day job working in an advertising agency, I was working all hours in the studio, and Stu was off doing gigs with the Stones. There was a convent school for girls just up the road and they would congregate in our driveway on the way home if the Stones' van was parked there. In those days girls would write on the van with lipstick, so it did not take long for the entire vehicle to be covered with messages of love and adulation for each member of the band. When the bodywork was covered they would write on the windows, so Stu would carry a crate of Coca-Cola in the back specifically for the purpose of cleaning the lipstick off so that he could see to drive.

By this time the Stones had a successful record deal and were being managed by Andrew Oldham, who had taken the decision to fire Stu from the band as he felt Stu did not look right. I thought that was pretty extraordinary as none of them were exactly textbook for a rock star. He was offered the job as their road manager, I am sure out of loyalty from some members of the band and also due to the fact that he owned the van that they all traveled in with the gear. I was in the next room at Decca Studios when he was told, and when I expressed my disgust at their decision he told me that he was quite happy with the arrangement, adding that the idea of being a pop star had no appeal to him whatsoever and, as he felt they would become incredibly successful, it would be a great way to see the world. As time went by, it proved to be an excellent decision, as he really took to his new role and the freedom it gave him. He was far too straight to ever be a rock star. The Stones were the true beneficiaries. They not only got the services of a great piano player, they also had the most trustworthy friend anyone could wish for as a road manager. Keith Richards has always said that he is still working for Stu and, as far as he is concerned, The Rolling Stones are Stu's Band.

. . .

Stu kept all the Stones' gear at the house, so we would appropriate guitar amps various from the loft in the roof to use for our sound system, which was very rarely silent, and incredibly loud. Fortunately, the house was in the middle of a large plot a long way back from the road and the neighbors on either side were some distance away. There were many great parties at "The Bungalow," with much coming and going. There was always something going on, but because we were all so busy we never seemed to get under each other's feet.

After some months, Brian Wiles, feeling left out of the action, decided he was going to become a singer and put a blues band together. Stu, being the pal that he was, took it upon himself to help, as Brian did not know any musicians other than those he met through Stu and me, and they were all committed to other bands. I thought the whole idea was a joke, having had the misfortune to hear Mr. Wiles sing, and a blues singer he was not. A few weeks went by and I was informed that the band was formed and ready to play their first gig. It was to be at a local folk club in Leatherhead on a Sunday afternoon. Dreading the prospect, I thought I should at least show willing and went.

Brian was as insipid as I had expected, but the guitar player was astonishing. I had never seen anything quite like him. Playing rhythm and lead seamlessly with a fantastic sound. He was very cool-looking, quite scruffy, and had car grease ingrained in his hands. I grabbed Stu and asked where the hell he had found this guy. He and Brian had gone to see a band called the Tridents at Eel Pie Island, a popular venue on an island in the middle of the Thames at Twickenham. Being impressed with the guitar player, they approached him after the gig and asked if he would consider joining Brian's new band, the Nightshift. Everyone knew who Stu was, and I am sure that that was the reason Jeff Beck agreed to join.

The band did not last long, but Stu and Jeff became lifelong friends and he quickly became one of the crowd that would hang out at the house, as he lived a short distance away in Carshalton. There must have been something in the water locally, as you could have thrown a net over the small area that Jimmy Page, Jeff Beck, Eric Clapton, and Stu came from.

STU AND THE STONES' VAN.

Norwegian Bird

Stu came home one day with a very pretty, young Norwegian girl he had found thumbing a lift on the side of the road. Apparently, she had been working for a local family as an au pair and had run away in search of some adventure. They spent the night together, and as he was leaving the following day for a six-week tour of America, he asked me to keep an eye on her until he got back home.

I did not relish the idea at all. Particularly as I was working six or seven days a week, a minimum of twelve hours a day. I didn't feel comfortable having her around or leaving her alone in the house for long periods of time. She definitely looked like trouble. However, Stu was my pal and I could not refuse his request. She must have made quite an impression on him.

Although physically very attractive, there was something slightly unbalanced about her. My initial impression quickly proved to be correct, with the exception of "slightly." A couple of days after Stu had gone, I came home to find her with her head in the gas oven with a half-empty bottle of vodka next to her on the floor. I have no idea if she waited until she heard me coming and leapt into position or not, but she certainly gave me one hell of a fright.

As I have said, I was very busy at the time, spending long hours in the studio, often not arriving home until dawn. One such morning I was about to put the key in the lock of the front door, when it swung open and there stood Jeff Beck. Somehow he had got wind of Stu's good fortune with his young Norwegian friend and, knowing that he was away, decided to take advantage of his absence. I warned Jeff off, saying he was a creep for going behind Stu's back and that I had better not catch him at the house again.

Many years later, while on the road with the ARMS tour, he told me, after that night, he would creep round the back of the house and climb into Stu's room through the window. Leaving undetected by the same route, very often with me asleep in the next room.

I don't think she even waited for Stu's return before she left. I certainly did not encourage her to stay and may well have facilitated her departure in some way. She was a total pain in the arse.

Stu was the great leveler for the band. He would always tell it like it is. There would be no posturing around him. No one was spared his frank and invariably hysterically funny opinion. Although they often appeared to take what he said with a pinch of salt, they knew that he wasn't going to bullshit them like everyone else around them, and I am sure that a lot of what he said and did had an extremely positive effect on the band as a whole and on the individuals in it. He would go to get them from the dressing room before each show when it was time for them to go onstage, saying, "Come along my little shower of shit." I am sure no one else on this planet has ever spoken to them like that since his untimely death in 1985.

He didn't approve entirely of the direction they took when they started writing their own material. He refused to play anything that he considered to have "Chinese," or minor, chords in it. That is, anything that was not the more traditional rhythm and blues or boogie-woogie format. So we had to get someone else in to play what he would not. He still played at every gig. He just played the songs that he wanted to.

The Stones have had a fantastic selection of great piano players perform with them over the years, the cream of the crop: Nicky Hopkins, who in my opinion was a genius, Chuck Leavell, Billy Preston, and Mac—Ian McLagan, the great rough-and-ready rock and roll keyboard player from the Small Faces and the Faces. All of these guys were specialists in their own style of playing and were all quite different from one another, but The Rolling Stones never swung like they did when Stu was playing with them. They became another band. The rhythm section became a whole other thing. The best I have ever heard. He had the most extraordinary feel that seemed to be in complete sympathy with Bill, Charlie, and Keith.

Stu was like no one else I have ever met. He did what he wanted, when he wanted. He had a rather selfish way of life, not at all in an unpleasant way, as he never interfered with anyone else. You always knew where you were with him. It made for an uncomplicated relationship. I consider him to have been the best friend I will ever have.

The one question that will always remain with me is, here we have a man who remained exactly the same as the day I met him, with all this total lunacy going on around him. Straight as a die. No drugs. Didn't smoke. Played golf. He has been dead for almost thirty years, and the band, some of whom have put themselves through the rigors of extreme abuse of one sort or another, are still at it. There is something wrong somewhere.

STU AND MICK, 1965.

To Continue '62

IBC Studios had been bought in late 1962 by Eric Robinson, then the head of Light Music at the BBC, and a musician associate of his named George Clouston, who was to run the place on a day-to-day basis. I quickly saw an opportunity and approached George with an idea that would enable me to start producing records using IBC, with me finding the talent and George providing the studio and the business expertise. I had no money and no track record, and in those days the idea of an engineer becoming a producer was unheard of. So I was not likely to be approached by any record company, and I was constantly coming across talent that I could do nothing about. It was a no-brainer. He had nothing to lose. I did all the work and all he had to do was let me use the studio during downtime. He agreed on the condition that he would have the sole freedom to place the artists I found with a label and that I would have no say in any of the business negotiations.

RED LION
SUTTON

R&B CLUB
rhythm and blues

with the
ROLLING STONES
alternate fridays
7·30 — 10·30
admission   members
4'-   3'-

A FLYER FOR THE ROLLING STONES' FIRST SHOW
AT THE RED LION.

The first act that I brought in was The Rolling Stones, in March 1963. I had started a rhythm and blues night with them at the Red Lion pub in Sutton on the alternate Friday to The Presidents, the band that I managed.

We had been running a club for our Gang on alternate Fridays for about a year, and it had become extremely popular. So Stu and I thought an R&B night would be a good thing to try. However, this did not prove to be the case. It was right at the beginning for the Stones, and only about a dozen people turned up for the first couple of gigs so we had to close it down. The arrangement was that we split the take on the door, so I shall go down in the annals of rock and roll history for paying the Stones the smallest fee ever for a gig. The equivalent of £3 for the night. This was before Bill Wyman and Charlie Watts had joined the band, with my pal Colin Golding playing bass and Tony Chapman on drums. They were already great, playing Howlin' Wolf, Jimmy Reed, and Bo Diddley covers. Music that very few people in Britain had heard. It seemed that they were ahead of their time for the locals in Surrey.

So some weeks later, after Bill and Charlie had joined the band, I approached Stu with the idea of me taking them into IBC to record them under my arrangement with George Clouston.

They turned up for the session with Brian being very much the leader of the band. He came into the control room to discuss what we were going to do, leaving me in no doubt as to who was in charge. I realize now that this was probably due to nerves, as none of them had ever seen the inside of a real studio before. Although I grew to have a huge respect for him as a musician, I took an instant dislike to him, which was to remain for some years.

We cut five songs that night: "Diddley Daddy" and "Road Runner," both Bo Diddley songs; "Baby, What's Wrong" and "Bright

Lights Big City" by Jimmy Reed; and Willie Dixon's "I Want to Be Loved." I thought the results were tremendous. I had finally got to record the music that had inspired me so much on my American pal Pat's Jimmy Reed album. They sounded like the real deal. I remember being particularly impressed by Brian Jones's harmonica playing, and the extraordinary feel and sound that Charlie and Bill got, and it goes without saying, Stu's piano playing.

The tapes were given to George Clouston. He, knowing nothing about the popular music of the day, took the masters to the one person he knew, the head of the classical division at Decca Records, who of course didn't understand one side of what he was listening to.

Three weeks later I was coming back from lunch, and out of the front door of IBC Studios came The Rolling Stones. They told me they had decided that they did not wish to be commercial and therefore did not want a record deal. They had met Andrew Oldham for the first time a few days earlier when he had offered to manage them, along with an agent called Eric Easton. Andrew asked whether they had made any commitments to anybody and they told him of their arrangement with IBC Studios and me. So he then told them to go to George Clouston and get out of the arrangement whatever it took, giving them the money to pay for the studio time, should that become necessary, knowing that would probably be all it would take to get them out of the deal. It should be pointed out that George had never seen them until this point and they did look like nothing he had ever witnessed, with their odd clothes, attitude, and long hair. He probably couldn't wait to get them out of his office and, having failed miserably to get any interest in a deal for them with a major label, felt pleased with himself for getting out of it with the cost of the studio time in his pocket.

The following week, Andrew Oldham took them to Regent sound

studios, and he took the recording to the right guy at Decca, and the rest is history.

I was quite convinced that they were going to be huge. Not just because of their music but because of their antiestablishment attitude and, of course, the way that they looked. I immediately started to grow my hair and change the way I dressed, much to my parents' dismay.

Once the record had been released and became an instant hit, each week I would take a copy of the *NME* and leave it on George's desk, open at the charts. Needless to say, I never forgave him for not consulting me before letting them go. I realized that my original idea had a fatal flaw, and that was George and his total inability to recognize anything remotely commercial, and of course his complete lack of faith in me.

Not long after the Stones' session, I had gone to the Flamingo Club in Soho to see Georgie Fame and the Blue Flames. This was one of the best venues in London for live music and had quite a reputation for its weekend all-nighters. It was run by the Gunnell brothers: the older Rik, who in his youth had been a successful amateur boxer, and John, who had this massive scar down one side of his face. I often wondered how he got it but never had the nerve to ask.

I've been told that in order to operate a music venue in the West End in the late fifties and early sixties, you had to get permission and pay dues to one of the East End gangs, most likely Ronnie and Reggie Kray's lot or maybe an infamous villain named Jack Spot. So most of the guys running clubs seemed to be on the edge of the law. The Gunnell brothers were always perfectly pleasant to me. In fact, they became clients, as they retained me to record a couple of the acts that they managed.

I had met Georgie several times before when he was the keyboard player for Billy Fury, England's answer to Elvis. So we knew each other and had always got on well. After the show I told him of my new arrangement at IBC and asked if he would care to come one evening with the band and record two or three songs on the understanding that we may be able to get him a record deal. He agreed to the idea and we made arrangements for the session to be in a few days' time. When he turned up, he brought Shel Talmy with him. Shel had evidently approached him, showing interest in producing him, so Georgie decided to kill two birds with one stone. I was not best pleased, to say the least. I had never met Shel and I had no idea who he was. I explained in no uncertain terms that it was my session and I was producing it. Shel remained calm and very politely suggested that, as we were both there, why did we not just get on with it and see how it goes. I begrudgingly agreed and it turned out to be one of the best decisions I ever made. I quickly came to realize that Shel knew what he was doing, and seemingly, he felt the same about me. We became great pals and started what was to become a very successful partnership, with me engineering most of the records that he produced over the next few years. These included "My Generation" by The Who, and "All Day and All of the Night" and "You Really Got Me" by The Kinks.

As far as I know, Georgie Fame never used the tapes to get himself a record deal. George Clouston let that one slip through his fingers as well, so I brought my arrangement with him to an end.

Late in 1963 I was to record Georgie Fame and the Blue Flames' first album, *Rhythm and Blues at the Flamingo*, with Sammy Samwell producing. Sammy knew I was a big fan of the Blue Flames, and as IBC had the only independent remote recording unit in England, I was an obvious choice for the job. The problem was, the Flamingo's band room was a rat-infested hole-in-the-wall next to the stage, and it was the only place I could set up the gear. By the time the 3-track Ampex machine, a console, and three large speakers were stuffed in there, there was barely room for me. I remember we hung a blanket in the doorway, as there was no door between the hole and the stage. From where I was sitting I could lean through it and touch Georgie sitting at the organ.

Unfortunately, Johnny McLaughlin and Speedy were not available that night. Johnny was so cool in his sharkskin suit and pencil tie with a button-down shirt. He would lean on the pillar on the left side of the stage, barely moving, while playing the most incredible guitar. So his place was taken at the last minute by Big Jim Sullivan, who, considering he did not know the material, did a wonderful job. Speedy, the conga player in the band, was in jail, having been busted for drugs, so his place was taken by a friend of Georgie and a regular at the Flamingo, Tommy Thomas. He did his best but it was not quite the same. Red Reece and Boots Slade were on drums and bass, and what an incredible rhythm section they were. The snare drum sound that Red got on that stage at the Flamingo was certainly one of the best I have ever heard. This is a great record and a fine example of Georgie Fame's extraordinary talent as a musician, bandleader, and singer.

Georgie Fame, or Clive Powell, which is his real name, went on to become a great friend, with me producing him in later years for Chris Blackwell's Island Records. He came and played with Charlie Watts and Eric Clapton at my second wedding. Now that was quite a band.

Nowadays he plays with his two talented sons as a trio and is a permanent member of Bill Wyman's band, The Rhythm Kings. I consider him to be one of the finest musicians I have ever had the pleasure of working with. He is an exceptional Hammond B3 player with a rare complete understanding of the instrument, and I love the sound of his voice, his jazz roots facilitating the most wonderful phrasing. He and Andy Fairweather Low are my two favorite bandleaders. Both have the extraordinary ability to seamlessly take control of a group of musicians without appearing to be bossy or superior in any way and within minutes have them all pointing in the same direction, with remarkable results.

Going Freelance

I made two more singles, in a dying attempt to become a successful singer. They were both produced by Tony Meehan, the ex-drummer of Cliff Richard's group The Shadows, the first massive pop group in the UK.

I did a cover of "I'll Follow the Sun" for Pye Records. Terry Johnson, who by then had left IBC for a job at Decca Studios, did a marvelous engineering job. Tony Meehan did a great arrangement, with strings, a French horn, woodwind, a great rhythm section, and the Mike Sammes Singers. No expense spared. I remember getting up on the day of the session and driving the hour and a half to Decca Studios without uttering a word, as I was convinced that my voice had a much better edge to it having not been used all night.

Once again it was a strange experience being on the other side of the glass with an orchestra and vocal group that I was used to seeing daily as an engineer. They were all very kind and encouraging, but yet again it came to nothing.

The second song, called "Mary Anne," was released on Immediate Records, and I decided to turn professional as a singer on its release. I left my job at IBC, believing that I'd gone as far as I could go. I had been the senior engineer at the studio for at least a year and the only other promotion I could expect would be to manage the place, which had no appeal whatsoever. Anyway, the whole idea of working at the studio in the first place was to learn about the business and to try to get discovered as a singer.

The reviews were quite encouraging. I did the usual promotion, a couple of TV shows and a handful of interviews in the music press. All to no avail. The record did not sell and within five or six weeks I was back at home twiddling my thumbs, realizing, among other things, that in order to be a successful singer you had to be able to remember the lyrics to a song. Something I had serious trouble with.

I had been very fortunate to acquire some really successful clients in the previous couple of years at IBC, the foremost of these being Shel Talmy. He had arrived in London and convinced the powers that be in the English record business that he was an established producer from Los Angeles. How accurate this was I never found out. I think he may have had a somewhat menial job at Capitol Studios in Los Angeles. The fact is, he had a string of hits straight out of the bag, so he was doing something right.

I was sitting at home one morning, wondering what would become of me, when the phone rang, and it was Shel. He said that he was having trouble finding anyone to replace me as an engineer and asked if I would consider going back to work at IBC. I told him I wouldn't under any circumstances, so he then suggested that he would pay me an hourly rate as a freelance.

I should point out that there was no such thing in the industry at the time, and the immediate question was whether the studios would even consider allowing an outsider to come in and use their facilities, putting out the noses of their employees. I rang George Clouston and put the idea to him. He tried to persuade me to take my old job back, without success. It seemed that business at IBC had subsided since I had left, so it didn't take much to convince him that I could return as a freelance, with the studio paying me by the hour for the clients that I brought in. So it is thanks to Shel that I returned to the fold and continued my career as an engineer, being paid both by the client and the studio and becoming the first freelance engineer in the business. I would most certainly never have come up with this concept myself and it was only Shel, pointing out the opportunity and facilitating it, who made it happen.

After a few months, the rest of the staff at IBC quite understandably rebelled and threatened to walk out if I was allowed to continue, as they were getting very little work. So I had to go and find another studio to use. As I was fortunate enough to have a very successful string of clients and artists, initially Pye Studios in Marble Arch and eventually Olympic Studios welcomed me with open arms.

The original Olympic Studios was just behind Baker Street. I only went there once or twice before the new Olympic opened in Barnes, south of Hammersmith Bridge in London. The first session I did there was for Andrew Oldham with Marianne Faithfull. I immediately fell in love with the place and it was to become my studio of choice in England for many years. And very happy years they were. Studio 1 became my second home and I was to record many of my favorite albums in this hallowed room. It was quite an amazing space. Incredibly versatile. You could record anything from a sixty-piece orchestra to the loudest rock and roll band in there and somehow it would adapt.

It was originally a cinema, and the conversion to a recording studio had been designed and built on a very small budget by Keith Grant, who ran the place until it was eventually sold many years later to Richard Branson. Keith was a fine engineer and was responsible for creating one of the best recording facilities in the world. Coincidentally, it was he who vacated his position at IBC that made way for me starting there in 1959. So I am indebted to him in more ways than one.

The other main contributor to the success of Olympic was Dick Swettenham. He designed all the recording consoles and so was responsible for the extraordinary recorded sound that the studio became famous for. Sad to say that both Keith and Dick are no longer with us. Certainly their passing represents the end of a wonderful era.

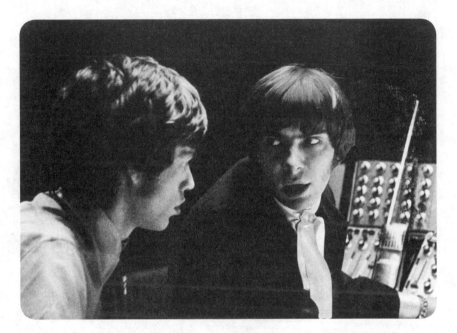

STONES SESSION AT OLYMPIC STUDIOS.

Andrew Oldham

About a year went by after the debacle of the first sessions with the Stones at IBC involving George Clouston and Andrew Oldham. I had maintained a firm friendship with the band and would go with them in the van with Stu to the odd gig, time allowing. They were already showing signs of the greatness to come as a rhythm section, with Mick and Keith having more influence and slowly taking the reins away from Brian.

Stu and I were living together by this time, and I had got over the fact that they had dumped me and IBC and gone with Andrew Oldham. This proved to be a very smart move on their part. As far as I am aware, Andrew had absolutely no knowledge of the process whatsoever, other than the Sunday session of mine that he had visited a couple of years before. But he had more front than Harrods and bluffed and barged his way through the bullshit of the business, having a complete disregard for the way things were normally done. His expertise was PR and it was this ability, in my opinion, that made him almost entirely responsible for the Stones' initial success. Mind you, he did have some extraordinary subjects to work with. The way they looked, played, and behaved making the job much easier.

I was working late one afternoon in studio A at IBC when I got a call from Angela who ran the booking office, saying that they had an emergency. She asked if I would do the studio a favor and stay after my session to do a vocal overdub for a new client who had just rung to make the booking. By now I had turned freelance and was always booked by the client, so this was most unusual. I asked who it was and she told me it was Andrew Oldham. My opinion of Andrew was still that he had no idea what he was doing and was riding his luck with the Stones, as far as producing records was concerned. So, coupled with the fact that he had stolen them from under my nose, I was not disposed to have anything to do with him. Angela explained that there was no one else left in the building to do the session, so could I, on this one occasion, do them a favor? As I had a huge crush on her, she used her well-oiled female wily ways, and I begrudgingly agreed.

My session finished at 10:30 p.m., and at 11:00 p.m. sharp Andrew arrived. I told him that I was not at all happy about doing the session, but as I had been coerced into it we had better get on with it and get on home.

It was a vocal overdub onto an existing backing track. I do not recall who the artist was, but I have to say that, much to my surprise, I was really impressed with Andrew's production. At the end of the session, when asked, I reluctantly told him so.

He went to the phone and called his secretary and told her to put copies of the last couple of records he had produced in a cab to be delivered to IBC. Poor girl, it was one o'clock in the morning. The records arrived. He played them for me and asked sarcastically if he had passed the test. I hated to admit it but I owned up to being surprisingly impressed. So he asked if I would engineer for him in the future and I agreed.

This led to several years of work for me, as Andrew started his own label, Immediate Records, with me recording many of its releases throughout its existence from 1965 to 1970. However, by far the most significant outcome was my recording the Stones from then until I quit during *Black and Blue* many years later.

I so very nearly declined that session with Andrew. Who knows what would have happened to my career if I had. Thank God for dear Angela's persuasive ways.

EARLY DAYS WITH ANDREW LOOG OLDHAM AT IBC.

WITH BILL WYMAN IN MADRID,
FEBRUARY 1967.

Bill Wyman, Spain, 1966

In 1965, Bill Wyman suggested that he and I form Freeway Music, a company to produce and manage artists. In 1966, he found a group called The End, and having produced a single with them, we set about trying to get them work. I say "we" but this is not an area I had much expertise in and anyway I was working flat out and had very little time to spare, so getting them work was left to Bill when he was not recording or gigging with the Stones.

The End introduced us to an Englishwoman who said she was working in Madrid and had made friends with two brothers who had a magazine publishing empire. They wanted to expand into the music business so had started their own record label in Spain. She said that they were serious players and felt sure that they would be interested in signing The End, particularly as they were managed by a member of The Rolling Stones. So a meeting was set up and I hopped on a plane to Madrid to check them and their company, Sonoplay, out.

They could not have been more charming and hospitable. The offices were most impressive and it looked like they were serious about their entry into the music business.

I played the single we had cut with The End and they agreed to release it on the condition that the band would come to Spain to promote it, hopefully bringing with them their famous manager.

As I was leaving, they asked if I had anything else that might interest them. It just so happened that, completely by chance, in a pocket of my briefcase, I had an acetate of a redundant single I had cut a few weeks earlier of me singing the Jagger/Richards song "Lady Jane."

I had recorded the original as an album track with the Stones and thought it would be a good song for me to cover for my next record. My producer Tony Meehan did a great arrangement for a string quartet and Spanish guitar and I got Brian Jones to play sitar. It was an interesting combination of instruments, and having finished the session at IBC we were all really pleased with the result, only to find out a couple of days later that someone else had covered it and was already booked on the weekly TV show *Ready Steady Go!* It was essential to get this plug if you were to have a hit in those days. So having been beaten to it, we dropped the idea of releasing it, with poor Tony having to swallow the cost of the session.

So I played Sonoplay the acetate, without saying that it was me in case they thought it was awful. They listened to the record, and much to my relief they loved it and asked if they could release it. So I had to confess. That did not put them off, and we negotiated a deal on the spot. I returned to England, feeling very pleased with myself, having got a check for the cost of the session to repay Tony Meehan, and thought no more about it.

Some months later The End had a tour of Spain booked to coincide with their record being released, and Bill and I decided it was time for him to go to Madrid to get some publicity for the band. Sonoplay was informed and the trip was booked.

Bill had been trying for some time to date a young Swedish lady he had met at the Bag O' Nails, a popular club he frequented in the West End of London. She was having none of it, which made him all the more determined to succeed. In one last attempt he asked her if she would like to come to Madrid for a few days. Initially she declined, and having spurned all previous attempts to get her attention, she finally capitulated and agreed to join him.

We met at Heathrow and he introduced me to the girl, telling me that as he was married, it would have to appear as if she was with me, should anyone ask in Madrid. That was all I needed. It was going to be busy enough without having her round our necks.

When the plane came to rest on the tarmac at Madrid airport, it was immediately obvious that Sonoplay had done a great PR job for Bill's arrival. The Rolling Stones had never played in Spain, so this was quite an event. The rooftop of the airport building was covered with screaming girls and the tarmac at the bottom of the stairs from the aircraft was littered with a heaving mass of journalists, photographers, film and TV cameramen, all jostling each other to get a better view of the passengers' exit from the plane.

I decided to go ahead of Bill, with the girl in tow behind me, and having got to the bottom of the aircraft steps, we moved away from the melee and stood under the wing of the plane. When I turned in order to watch Bill's exit, I realized that the paparazzi had followed me and were furiously snapping away, taking pictures of me and the girl. I figured that they had mistaken me for Bill, as I had long hair. At the back of the crowd I picked out the rep from Sonoplay and shouted to him to tell these idiots they were taking pictures of the

B-SIDE COVER FOR THE FOLLOW-UP SINGLE
FOR SONOPLAY IN SPAIN, 1967.

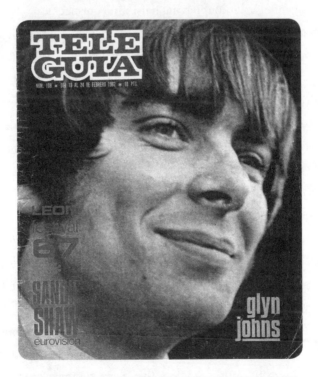

I ONLY GOT ON THE COVER OF THIS MAGAZINE
BECAUSE THE RECORD COMPANY OWNED IT.

wrong guy and that Bill was coming down the steps as I spoke. He called back, saying, "No, no, they are taking pictures of the right guy. Your record 'Lady Jane' is number one." This came as quite a shock as I had no idea that it had even been released, and in fact I had forgotten all about it.

We fought our way out of the airport and drove to a hotel in the middle of Madrid, checked in and went to our respective rooms to settle in and unpack. After about ten minutes, my phone rang. It was Bill. "'Ere, she wants her own room. She's locked herself in the bathroom and won't come out." I said that there was little I could do about it, and suggested he put her on a plane back to London, as it was obvious that she was just going to be a complete pain in the arse.

Two minutes later, my phone rang again and it was her. Still locked in the bathroom, she said she had no intention of sleeping with Bill and asked if she could come to my room instead. I declined, adding that surely she had not been so naive as to expect her own room when she accepted the invitation.

The trip was a success. Bill and I had a great time, with him being feted around Madrid. We even had dinner with El Cordobés, the legendary bullfighter, who seemed to have the status of Elvis in Spain. He was charming and excellent company, giving Bill the most beautiful embroidered bullfighter's jacket.

The band got the publicity it needed, I did a couple of gigs with them and a whole load of press and TV to promote my record, and returned to obscurity in the UK. I have no idea which chart the guy from Sonoplay was referring to. I think he may have been overexcited and exaggerated a bit. Bill ended up winning over the girl and must have made quite an impression on her in the process, as he and Astrid Lundström spent the next sixteen years together.

Managers in the Early Sixties

The music business in the early sixties was a bit like the Wild West, or a video game. Every day was spent zigzagging and ducking, trying to avoid the unsavory individuals that the business was littered with. It attracted every kind of dodgy character you could imagine. Hanging around on the fringes like vultures on a fence, waiting to swoop on unsuspecting naive young musicians.

There is no official qualification to become a manager, other than the ability to spot talent and convince them that you could further their career by representing them. To be fair, many of these guys were invaluable, and because of their expertise and contacts were able to successfully steer artists up the ladder by motivating the record company and creating a strategy of promotion that resulted in far greater success than perhaps the artists deserved, while saving them far more than the manager's commission came to.

However, there were many more who took advantage in the early days and worked the acts incredibly hard, seeming to have no concern for their well-being or bank balance. Perhaps the best known of these was Don Arden. He managed the Small Faces among others, and as I was engineering their records I got to know him quite well. Initially he seemed fine to me. He always paid my invoices promptly, and as he represented several other acts, he used me on other occasions to record them for his production company.

I went to *Ready Steady Go!* one Friday to supervise the sound for an appearance of the Small Faces. After the show, Ronnie Lane passed out in the dressing room from exhaustion. They had been on the road solidly for weeks, sometimes doing two shows a night with long distances to travel in between. This had taken its toll on them all, and they were pretty wiped out. I put Ronnie in my car and drove him back to the house I shared with Stu in Epsom. He stayed a couple of nights with no one knowing where he was and got to rest up and recover.

Ronnie and I had always got on well but this time together cemented what was to become a great friendship. He was the only person to sit me down and tell me to my face where I was at fault and take me to task about my sometimes acerbic personality. He nicknamed me "Bluto," after the bully in the comic strip *Popeye*. No one in the band was bigger than five-foot-seven, so as I was six feet they were easy to intimidate.

They became more and more frustrated with Don Arden's management and asked me to speak to Andrew Oldham on their behalf, to see if he would be interested in managing them and signing them to Immediate Records.

Andrew had meetings with them and Don Arden, and after the exchange of £25,000 in cash in a brown paper bag, the band were somehow set free from their contract with Decca Records and Arden's management. As Don was well known for threatening violence in order to get his own way, I am amazed that Andrew managed this coup with a simple cash transaction without some serious unpleasantness. All I know is that Arden blamed me for being part of the conspiracy to get the Small Faces away from him, when all I had done was introduce them to Andrew Oldham at their request.

Sometime later I was in Madrid, where I met a young singer who told me she had just signed with Arden. I foolishly told her she had made a big mistake, as he was not to be trusted. She went back to London and told him what I had said.

When I returned to London, a man named Reg, who used to work for Andrew Oldham as his driver and bodyguard, contacted me, saying that he had a band that I should see with the view to making a record. We arranged to meet one evening at Olympic Studios while I was on a break in my session.

As the office at the studio was locked, there was nowhere private to chat, so he suggested that we go outside to his car. I readily agreed, having no idea what I was about to be confronted with.

The car was an Aston Martin and there was another man sitting in the driver's seat. Reg invited me to sit in the back and then got into the passenger seat in the front. They both turned to face me in the back and I immediately recognized the second guy as a small-time club owner who I had had several run-ins with in the past when I was managing The Presidents. We frequently played his venue and he would never pay the agreed fee. I would always argue, knowing that, as the police station was opposite, there was little chance of it turning too violent. He was a short, stocky man and apparently had been a professional wrestler. He always had a huge sidekick, with the high-pitched voice of a eunuch, on the door. They made a very odd couple. I never liked him, and as it turned out, the feeling was mutual, because when he turned round in the car, he leveled a sawn-off shotgun at me.

Reg told me that Don Arden had sent them. That their instructions were to shoot me in the legs, but as they both knew me—Reg claiming that he even liked me—they were just going to issue a warning, and that I was to attend a meeting the following week at Don Arden's office without fail or they would carry out their employer's original request.

I sat rigid in shock until I came to my senses and realized that it was all for show, and I nervously suggested that he put the gun away because he clearly was not going to use it in his car as it would make quite a mess.

Having been summoned to a meeting, I realized that it was not going to be at all pleasant. I informed my friends Shel Talmy and Sammy Samwell—who was supposedly well connected—what was going on. They both told me to ring as soon as the meeting was over and that if they had not heard from me within a reasonable length of time, they would notify the police. I made a point of mentioning this as I was ushered into Arden's office by a large minder, who stood at the back of the room with his sleeves rolled up. I had seen this guy around, as he was involved with running a few dance halls in South London and was usually accompanied by an enormous Alsatian dog. Don—a short, stocky, unattractive man—sat behind a huge desk, I suppose to increase his feeling of self-importance. He had definitely seen too many Edward G. Robinson movies.

He told me that if I ever mentioned his name again it would not matter where I was or what I was doing, he would find me and shoot me and my family. A bit over-the-top considering all I had done was inform someone quite accurately that he was not to be trusted. I said nothing and left, feeling extremely relieved to get out of the building in one piece.

There were many stories about Don, none of them pleasant. He intimidated the artists he represented, and anyone else who got in his way. He supposedly had someone blow out the windows of Steve Marriott's house with a shotgun, and he is most famous for supposedly having a man hung out of a third-story window by his ankles. He eventually moved to Los Angeles, where I am told he lived in a mansion with armed guards everywhere. I suspect that this paranoia was as a result of him trying his strong-arm tactics on the wrong guys in America and coming up against the real thing. Years later I met his daughter, Sharon Osbourne, who was fabulous, bright, and interesting, seemingly not inheriting any of her father's unpleasant attributes.

Chris Blackwell

Perhaps the most extraordinary man I have ever met in the music business is Chris Blackwell, the founder of Island Records. He started his label in Jamaica in 1959 and established it in London in 1962, being one of the very first to start an independent record company.

Our first meeting was at IBC in 1964. The session was to record Millie singing "My Boy Lollipop" on a track he had previously recorded elsewhere. The record went on to sell more than six million copies. Not a bad start for his first production in England. He had cut his teeth as a producer in Jamaica, having built a small studio in a shack and recording local talent.

He was softly spoken, always casually dressed, with a cultured English accent and an air of relaxed confidence about him that was extremely reassuring. You were never left in doubt that he was in charge or that he knew exactly what he was doing, but this was achieved in an extremely pleasant, unchallenging, seemingly egoless fashion.

He proved over and over again that he had exceptional taste in music and played an enormous roll in dictating what would become successful from the late sixties until the sale of Island Records in 1998.

The list of talent he signed and sometimes produced is too long to mention here, but here are a few: Bob Marley, U2, The Cranberries, PJ Harvey, The Spencer Davis Group, Traffic, Steve Winwood, Cat Stevens, and Fairport Convention.

He could spot talent a mile off. Then he would support it, within reason, come what may. This made his label a target for many artists. There is a huge element of security if you are signed to a label by the guy who owns it. The same was true of A&M, in my experience. Jerry Moss was always supportive and loyal to his artists. Whereas, if you were signed by an employee of a major label, who was to say how long he or she would be in the job and who would replace them should they leave.

I believe Chris's finest skill is as a negotiator. I would pit him against any of the heavy hitters I have come across in the business. He has this extraordinary ability of coming at a problem from a completely different angle than expected, catching his opponent un-awares and unprepared, invariably getting the upper hand.

In the summer of 1968 he asked me if I would help him design a studio that he intended to build in Notting Hill. He had acquired a building in Basing Street that had been a church and was pretty der-elict, perfect for a complete interior refit. There were to be two stu-dios, one above the other, and office space on top of that. We had several meetings over the next few months, but I was unable to contribute fully to the project as I was incredibly busy working. Chris was extremely understanding and seemed quite happy to have my input as and when I was around. My major contribution was suggesting that he form a company with Dick Swettenham for the purpose of designing and building the consoles. I persuaded Dick to leave Olympic, which he was happy to do, being given the opportunity to start his own company with Chris backing it. The resulting consoles were a great success and Helios went on to establish itself all over the world.

The first time I used the studio was in June 1970 to mix The Band's *Stage Fright* album. This was the first 16-track recording I ever came across, and Basing Street, having just been built, was one of the first studios in London to acquire a 16-track machine, so I had little choice. Fortunately, the studio with its Helios console proved to be a great combination.

Todd Rundgren had engineered the record and Levon Helm came up with the idea that I should mix it. Robbie Robertson quite understandably wanted Todd to mix what he had started. So there was a standoff that resulted in Todd coming to London with the multitrack tapes and he and I doing our own set of mixes independently. We never even met. He would send me a reel of masters, and when I had finished he would have it collected and another reel would arrive for me to work on. I was disappointed that none of the band were able to attend the sessions. It was the first time I had ever mixed anything without the artist being present. This was doubly strange, as I had never heard the material before and I was used to getting the approval of the artist by running by any ideas I had to change the sound or arrangement before committing them to a mix. Once I got used to the idea I really enjoyed it.

Levon was very happy with the mixes I sent and I still don't really know how many of mine got used. I hope it was fifty-fifty. That would seem fair. I have a great deal of respect for Todd and hope he was not too upset with me messing with his recordings. If the roles had been reversed, I would not have dealt with it well. I had been a huge fan of The Band ever since their first album, *Music from Big Pink*, which came out in 1968 and had a massive influence on me, so it was a particular thrill to be asked to work with them.

The next time I used Basing Street was in August 1970 to mix *Get Yer Ya-Ya's Out!*, the Stones' live album that I had recorded at Madison Square Garden in New York and the Civic Center in Baltimore in November 1969. This was the second occasion that I had mixed a record without the artist being present and the only time I can remember it happening with the Stones, as Mick and Keith always took a very active part in the mixing process. Of course, they checked and approved what I had done before we mastered it.

At the beginning of 1971 I mixed Graham Nash's solo album *Songs for Beginners* at Basing Street. What a fabulous record that was. He was definitely at his peak as a songwriter. Crosby, Stills, Nash & Young had previously approached me to work with them on *Déjà Vu* in 1969, but I had heard that they were all at each other's throats so I declined. I had met Graham a couple of times in the sixties when he was in The Hollies and I was a big fan. What a great band they were. I have always felt really proud of Graham for being recognized for the British talent that he is and being accepted as an equal into the great American popular music tradition, and quite rightly so. You won't meet a nicer guy. He is generous to a fault and a true professional to work with.

The first album I made in its entirety at Basing Street was the Eagles' *Desperado*.

SITTING ON THE BACK OF THE TRUCK BACKSTAGE
AT MADISON SQUARE GARDEN.

RECORDING *YA YA'S* AT MADISON SQUARE GARDEN.

. . .

In 1976, Chris decided to build a studio near his house in Nassau, in the Bahamas. He invited me to join him there to discuss forming a company to include the studio and accommodation for artists and musicians. I had a wonderful few days staying with Chris and discussing the details of what we were about to embark on. One of the other houseguests was Abe Somer, the most prestigious music business lawyer in Los Angeles. Abe grew up with my pal David Anderle and represented Jerry Moss, A&M Records, and The Rolling Stones, among many other heavy hitters. I had known him and his family socially for some time. He asked why I was staying with Blackwell, and when I told him of the studio project in Nassau he took me outside, sat me down, and told me I was making a big mistake by going into business with a friend. I told him that was exactly why I wanted to do it, because Chris was my friend.

Chris and I discussed a deal, and I was very happy to accept what I thought was an incredibly generous offer on his part. I met with the architect and we began the basic plans for the studio.

A few months later, Chris came to London and we met up again on a glorious sunny English day at Chris's house in Theale, near Newbury. The meeting went well until Chris told me that the deal he had originally offered had to change as the Bahamian government had insisted on one of its members being on the board as a director. I was not happy about what I considered to be corruption and having what Chris and I had originally agreed on substantially changed. So I politely withdrew.

Chris really did not need me and he went ahead with the project. Compass Point Studios opened in 1976 and became a great success. Stu and I went down for the opening to check it out, resulting in the

Stones recording there shortly thereafter. I returned whenever I could, and although I did not make any really successful records there, I always had a great time. Chris would let me stay in his guesthouse whether he was on the island or not, and when I remarried he kindly invited me and my second wife to stay as part of our honeymoon, very generously giving us his Boston Whaler boat as a wedding present. For many years I have had the registration plate LP1 on my cars and Chris had renamed the boat *El Pee One*, much to everyone's amusement.

The last project that I did there was in the mid-nineties with Belly, a great young band from Boston, with the gorgeous lead singer Tanya Donelly. We used Jack Puig to engineer and what an excellent job he did. It was a wonderful environment and was perfect if you needed to get away and work without distraction.

Once the studio was well established, Chris diversified into property, being largely responsible for the rejuvenation of Miami Beach in Florida and building hotels in the Bahamas. In 1989 he sold Island Records to Universal and he expanded his hotel business to Jamaica, and the record business lost one of its most influential entrepreneurs.

Let's Spend the Night Together, 1966

By now it was quite normal to have sessions go all night, a habit started by the Stones in 1966 while we were making *Between the Buttons*, with almost every session starting at 8:00 p.m. and going till 7:30 or 8:00 the following morning. On a Sunday afternoon in studio 1 at Olympic, we were recording Mick Jagger's vocal on "Let's Spend the Night Together." The track had already been recorded, so there was just Mick, Andrew Oldham, his driver Eddie, me, and my assistant in the studio. I had set up an open-fronted vocal booth a third of the way down the studio, facing the control room. We had been working for about twenty minutes and Mick was getting close to the take that we would eventually use.

He had lit up a joint, so there was a haze of blue smoke hanging above him. We were in the middle of a take when much to our surprise the main door into the studio opened and two uniformed policemen gingerly entered. The studio was one floor above street level.

ANDREW OLDHAM PRODUCING THE STONES AT OLYMPIC.

The policemen had been on their rounds of the area on foot, had tried the front door of the building, and finding it unlocked, came in to check it out. There being no one on the ground floor, they came up the large stone stairs to check the rest of the building, opened the meat locker door handle and pushed open the large soundproof door, walking straight into studio 1 and our session. The door was positioned well behind the booth I had built so they could not see Mick, had no idea who they were intruding on, and could only hear him singing. Mick in turn could not see them and was oblivious to their presence.

Andrew Oldham and I could see the boys in blue, and his reaction to the situation was remarkable, not only by the speed with which he reacted but by the extraordinary distraction he created to preserve Mick and himself from a certain bust. He asked me to stop the tape, with Mick in full voice. He told his ever-faithful driver Eddie to make a quick exit out of the back of the control room with his doctor's bag full of illegal substances various, then immediately put the talk-back key down to the studio, politely asking if he could help the two bewildered coppers standing at the back of the room. This informed Mick that we had company, and it was not until he peered round the screens to see what the hell was going on that they realized who it was they had interrupted, and in turn he realized the significance of who was standing there and that this could be quite a serious problem.

Andrew was up and out into the studio before you could say "jackrabbit." The policemen apologized for interrupting and explained how they happened to be there, thinking that the building might be being burgled. When Andrew saw how starstruck they had become he decided to have a little fun. After a brief polite conversation, he asked if they had their nightsticks with them, and when they

WAITING FOR KEITH. OLYMPIC, 1970.

were produced from down their trouser legs he asked if we could borrow them for a minute. Fascinated and somewhat overawed by Mick Jagger's presence, they readily agreed. Andrew passed them to Mick, saying that we needed some percussion on the bridge of the song. The two nightsticks sounded similar to claves when banged together. The policemen stood to one side, I ran the tape, and Mick overdubbed their truncheons on the bridge. They seemed thrilled by the experience, and having a great story to tell their kids, they left the building happy. When they had gone, the front door was locked, Eddie was summoned, and we continued, finishing the song that evening. For some extraordinary reason, Andrew and Mick decided to keep the totally unnecessary sound of the truncheons being hit together in the mix. If you listen carefully you can just hear them.

A typical session with the Stones would start at eight in the evening. I would get to the studio at around 7:15 and invariably find Charlie waiting patiently in the control room. A few minutes later we would be joined by Bill, both as regular as clockwork, always ready to play at the appointed time. Mick and Brian would arrive at around eight and then it was just a matter of waiting for Keith. This delay could be anything from half an hour to six in the morning. No one ever said anything, knowing it was pointless and accepting this as the status quo. We would get on as best we could until he arrived, reviewing what we had been doing or overdubbing Mick or Brian on tracks that required more work.

In the early days, Brian's ability to get a tune out of almost any instrument that was lying around the studio contributed enormously to the variety of the sound of the band, playing the recorder on "Ruby Tuesday" or finding a set of marimbas left by a session percussionist and coming up with the part for "Under My Thumb" that relentlessly drove the song. Brian was the king of the riff, "The Last Time" being a classic example, although it was Keith that came up with the instantly recognizable line for "Satisfaction." Neither would be considered a lead guitarist, so there was rarely any improvisation, with everything worked out to the last note, and Brian complementing Keith's exceptional rhythm with a variety of sounds.

Mick and Keith very often used the studio to write. One or the other would turn up with the bare bones of an idea. Typically, Keith might have a few bars of a chord sequence that he would sit and play over and over again for hours on end, with Bill and Charlie playing along, providing invaluable support with an extraordinary degree of patience. Brian and either Stu or Nicky Hopkins would join in, trying different ideas and instrumentation. As the song took shape, Mick would leave the control room, where he had been paying attention to the sound with me, and join in, singing along, developing a melody while muttering the odd word of nonsensical lyric. Eventually I would start recording and playing back their efforts in order for all involved to refine what they were doing under strict direction from Mick and Keith and either Andrew Oldham or, later, Jimmy Miller. This process would have been fascinating to be part of if it hadn't taken so long. Very often the adrenaline rush and excitement of what they were creating had long since evaporated by the time we arrived at a take that was acceptable to Keith. As absurd as this sounds, there were many occasions where earlier takes were far better than the master that was chosen. However, this did not seem to adversely affect the popularity of the song in question. The point I make is, they were even better than some of their records would suggest.

All Keith wanted to do was play. The only communication with me was in the form of a negative comment if he did not like some aspect of the sound. I knew everything was okay if he said nothing. In all the years I worked for them, he never said hello or good-bye or showed any interest in my well-being, as he had absolutely no interest in small talk. His living in a chemically induced state was the norm, so I never took it personally.

Although Andrew Oldham and then Jimmy Miller did a sterling job creating the environment for the band to work in and certainly contributed to the production, Mick and Keith really produced the records they made. Jimmy would sit in his chair smoking huge spliffs all night, rocking backward and forward in time to the music. He had excellent judgment of feel and sound and was a pleasure to work with but on occasion was too stoned to be of constructive use.

Andrew quit as the band's producer during the making of *Their Satanic Majesties Request,* jumping from what had already become a rudderless ship.

The bottom of the pit came one evening when I arrived to find two huge flight cases of percussion instruments being delivered to the studio. As each member of the band arrived, they were instructed by Mick to choose something from the large selection. Having randomly decided on a tempo, they proceeded to hit, shake, or scrape percussion with no shape or sequence or any other form of musical accompaniment. Each take, lasting anything up to fifteen minutes, would then be played back and scrutinized, and yet another would be done, identical in its chaos to all the others until they got bored and accepted one as a master. This became the unadulterated drivel that was "Sing This All Together." Not their finest hour.

When the pain of *Satanic Majesties Request* had finally subsided, Mick told me that they had decided to go back to using a producer and that they wanted an American. I shuddered at the thought of some unknown-quantity Yank coming in with ego and guns blazing, telling me how to do my job. A few weeks earlier I had met Jimmy Miller, who was working with Traffic in the next studio to me at Olympic. He seemed like a really nice guy and was doing a great job, so I told Mick that he did not have to import anyone as there was already an extremely accomplished guy in London. Mick and Keith checked him out and he got the job. Never knowing that it was me who recommended him, the first thing he did was replace me with Eddie Kramer to engineer. Fortunately this only lasted a few days before the band insisted on bringing me back.

While Keith, Charlie, and Bill drove the band rhythmically, Mick's energy and intellect drove everything else. I was constantly amazed by his skill as a songwriter and by the extraordinary energy he managed to summon for his vocal performances in the studio.

Both Mick and Keith would take an active part in the mixing process and drove me nuts making me mix a track for hours when I felt I had got it in the first couple of passes. We certainly did not always agree. I guess it would have been even more boring if we had. There were a couple of occasions when finally putting the album together I would play back earlier mixes that I had done on my own, to compare with the one they had chosen after hours of farting around, and in the cold light of day they would agree that mine were better. Equally, there were many occasions when they insisted on me changing a mix quite drastically from the way I heard it, with great effect.

Working with the Stones for all those years certainly had some amazing moments and I am proud to have been associated with them during a period of time when their music was so influential. However, Charlie summed it up perfectly when asked in a recent interview his experience of being in the band for fifty years. He replied, "Ten years of working and forty years of hanging around."

Stones European Tour,
Spring 1967

So, this was the first tour the Stones had done since Keith had stolen Brian's girlfriend, Anita Pallenberg, along with his chauffeur, Tom Keylock. In fact, I doubt if they had seen each other or even spoken to each other since that event.

We were all told to meet up at the check-in desk at Heathrow to collect our tickets prior to boarding the flight to Stockholm for the first gig. As I walked up to the assembled melee in front of the desk, Mick approached me, took me to one side, and asked if I would carry his stash for him. After getting a brusque refusal from me, he looked around for an alternative. Brian was the next to arrive, so Mick made a beeline for him and asked him the same question. Brian agreed, took the small silver package, and shoved it down his trousers into his underpants. I can only think this was in order to ingratiate himself to Mick.

We arrived at Stockholm airport and made our way through immigration to the customs hall. There, we were greeted by what appeared to be the entire Swedish media. The customs officers were waiting behind a long, low metal table and behind them stood a wall of film, still and TV cameras. The Swedish government had decided to use the Stones' arrival to send a message about its intolerance to drugs. It looked like they had gone to a great deal of trouble, setting up the customs hall so as to allow the best possible view for the cameras and reporters. Not at all the reception the band had envisaged.

One by one we were stood in front of a customs officer with our bags placed in front of us on the shiny metal–covered bench. The tour was to last several weeks, so as you can imagine, there was an immense amount of luggage to go through. Stu and I and Tom Keylock were dealt with very quickly. They were not very interested in us and anyway we had very little luggage in comparison to the band, who had stage finery by the trunkload to go through. Once they were finished with us, we sat on our bags about fifteen yards away, watching the band being searched in front of us. Brian hung back. The others all left the customs area immediately after they were finished with. So after a while he was the only one left. He stood there, a rather pathetic figure, with much of the color drained from his face, nervously shifting from one foot to the other while a team of customs men went through his stuff. I told Stu and Tom what he had down his underpants, so the three of us sat and nervously waited with bated breath. Suddenly Tom nudged me and whispered, "Look, down by his feet," and there, on the floor where Brian stood, was the little silver package, in full view to us on our side of the bench. It had slipped, accidentally or not, out of his underpants, down the inside of his trousers, and was now in full view. Tom got up and casually strolled over to Brian, put his hand on his shoulder as if to comfort him, engaged him in conversation, and calmly bent down and picked up the offending package, put it in his pocket, and returned to where we were sitting. Whereupon we decided to make our exit, knowing Brian was now going to be okay. The route from the customs hall out to the main concourse was a long corridor with potted palms on either side. It seemed to take an eternity as we attempted to walk casually along it, trying to look like we had not a care in the world, Tom having deposited the package in one of the pots.

Tom now had the job of head of security. Brian spent the rest of the tour separated from the band. He was not in good shape anyway, his problems with drugs and alcohol having taken their toll to such an extent that he could hardly hold a chord down on a guitar. The innovative input he originally contributed to the band had all but disappeared. The worse he got the less anyone wanted to have anything to do with him. He became isolated and quite lonely. I must say I felt sorry for him in the end, although I suppose he only had himself to blame.

A few days later, Stu and I were traveling from Denmark to northern Germany with all the Stones' gear in the back of an ordinary VW van. The day we left England the starter motor broke. So every time we had to start the van, I had to push it, while Stu sat in the driver's seat and steered. By the time we got to the ferry to cross from Sweden to Germany, I had this down to a fine art and we could start the van in a very few yards. Which was essential on a packed ferry.

As we drove south toward the coast, Stu's mood visibly darkened for no apparent reason. On arrival at the ferry, we boarded and went straight to the first-class restaurant for lunch, during which Stu's mood continued to plummet. I couldn't understand it. When we finished eating, he asked the young German waiter for the bill in an extremely surly manner, and it was duly brought. Stu took out his enormously thick leather wallet from its lifelong resting place in the permanently stretched hip pocket of his jeans, grabbed the bill, and while counting out the precise amount written on it, announced to the waiter, "You're not getting any more than this. Because of you lot, I didn't get any bananas until I was seven." I collapsed under the table in hysterics. The poor, unfortunate youth got the brunt of Stu's hangover from his childhood in the war. He had been boiling over all morning at the thought of having to go to Germany. The waiter had no idea what Stu was talking about and simply stood there in amazement until summarily dismissed.

The ferry docked and we drove off, having completed our well-rehearsed "push start" routine, much to the amusement of the deckhands. Now, as we were taking equipment into and then out of Germany, we had a carnet. This is an official commercial document for customs purposes with an extremely accurate and detailed description of every item on the van, which is checked as you leave the country to make sure you leave with exactly what you arrived with. This, in our view, made us the equivalent of a commercial vehicle. As we came off the ferry there were two lines of vehicles to the customs and immigration area—one for cars and one for trucks or commercial vehicles. The line for cars was extremely long and the line for trucks was empty. So we proceeded down past the long line of cars to an immigration official standing outside his little hut. I should say at this point that this was a man of extremely stunted growth, and like so many of his counterparts he was a textbook example of a small man with a power complex. He stepped out of his little shed, waving his stubby little arms. "Go back. Go back!" he screamed in German. Stu pulled up alongside him, already amused by the sight of an extremely upset German. There ensued a conversation about the rights and wrongs of us being in the line that we were in, with Stu speaking in English and the overexcited German in his native tongue. The long and the short of it was, we were made to return to the end of the private-car queue until we eventually reached the same official some ten or fifteen minutes later. He walked round to Stu's window and demanded our passports and disappeared with them. Meanwhile, Stu and I went into the customs office with the carnet. Behind a waist-high counter were standing two jackbooted customs guys. They took the carnet from Stu and were in the process of inspecting it when through the door burst our stunted friend with his superior officer who stood in the middle of the room, scrambled egg up his arm and on his cap, and proceeded to berate Stu in German while waving our passports in the air. I have no idea what the literal translation is but the gist of it was that he had received a complaint from his sawn-off compatriot about our attitude. He gave Stu back our passports and told us to go back the way we came. Stu opened his passport and noticed a stamp in it that he did not recognize. He asked in English what it meant, only to be told that he would find out when he got back to Denmark and that he should not come to Germany unless he could speak the language. So Stu demanded to know what was in his passport and said that he wasn't going anywhere until he had been told. He wasn't rude, he was firm, and much to my surprise he began speaking in fluent German. At this point the vertically challenged one leapt across the room, nightstick in hand, and tried to beat Stu over the head. However, Stu was too quick for him. He grabbed the guy's wrist to prevent him from striking, and continued to address the senior officer as if nothing was amiss, with the diminutive German flailing around on the end of Stu's arm like a rag doll. Pandemonium broke out. The two jackbooted gentlemen came from behind the counter with the speed of light. They stood on either side of me and in one seamless movement shoved a pistol up my nose, picked me up, took me outside, and placed me in the van, with me all the time calling in an ever higher pitch, "Stu, Stu, *Stu*." Meanwhile, Stu hadn't moved an inch. He was immensely strong and throughout this episode seemed to remain completely calm. The commander of the post was screaming at him, as was the guy on the end of his arm, while Stu continued to quietly demand in German to know what the stamp in his passport meant.

I don't mind admitting I was very frightened. I called out to Stu to "let it go"—both his demand to know what the stamp meant and the immigration officer—and to get into the van so we could leave before the situation got any worse. So he quietly let go of the German official and walked slowly to the van without saying a word, got in, and—with me pushing from behind—started the engine, turned the van around, and drove back to the ferry.

We returned to Denmark, checked into a hotel, and Stu got on the phone to the promoter in Hamburg to let him know that he had a bit of a problem. The concert was the following night. We had all the gear and it transpired that the stamp in our passports meant that we could never return to Germany.

Apparently, there were phone calls back and forth all night long between the promoter and the customs post, until finally Stu received a call from the promoter saying that if I was prepared to apologize to the commanding officer of the post in precise terms for what I had said to the immigration officer then he would let us back into Germany.

Now, I had long hair. Stu had an ordinary haircut. In fact, you would never even know Stu was a musician of any sort by looking at him. So when he gave me this message we both thought that it was because of my appearance that I was accused of being the trouble-maker. I had assumed that we had been thrown out because of Stu's argument and fight in the customs area. The more we thought about it the more confused we became. So Stu rang the promoter back and asked if he was sure that it was me who had to apologize and not him. Five minutes later we got a call back to say it was definitely me, the one with the long hair who had called the immigration officer a German bastard! Then I remembered that when we first arrived and the immigration guy sent us back to the end of the other queue, I had turned to Stu and muttered, "Kraut . . ." I have no idea how he heard me, if in fact he heard me at all, since the windows of the van were closed. Perhaps he was good at reading lips. Evidently that was what the whole episode had been about.

It was still very early in the morning. We returned to the ferry and took the short crossing back to Germany and in no time at all I was standing in this guy's office, where I was required to say, "I am sorry I called your officer a German bastard." Which wasn't too difficult at all.

We drove to Hamburg to meet up with the band and then the thirty miles on to Bremen, arriving in plenty of time for the concert. The auditorium was full of armed police, both backstage and out front. It was obvious that they were expecting trouble and were determined to stop anything before it happened. It was most unsettling. There was a line of police all around the interior of the auditorium and along the front of the stage with their rifles shouldered. Anytime a kid moved in the audience they were jumped on and roughly removed by a gang of police officers. Mick made several attempts at trying to calm things down, telling the police to be cool and not to be so violent. He had to be careful, as the crowd would have taken very little encouragement to riot as a result of the bully tactics that were being employed. He went up in my estimation enormously that night. He dealt with a tinderbox situation quite brilliantly.

Anyone who has been to a Rolling Stones concert will know that the experience is about as stimulating to all your senses as great rock and roll is ever likely to get. It is almost impossible to sit still with that many decibels of hit after hit being beamed at you, along with the realization that you are actually in the same room with THEM, or HIM, depending on your point of view, and they are playing just for you. So it can be very difficult to control your excitement. In fact, with most people, the whole idea of going is to let loose a bit. Well, this was not what the German police had in mind.

There was a certain point in the act when Mick would take a large basket of flowers and throw them by the handful to an already over-excited audience. This would cause chaos every night with kids climbing over one another, trying to catch a flying bloom. Mick, realizing that this could cause severe maiming or death to innocent kids at the hands of the gestapo, took the basket and slowly walked along the front of the stage, placing a rose down the barrel of each policeman's gun. He then turned back along the line and gave a flower to each one, pointing at the kid he was to give it to. In one stroke, he managed to compromise the police and dispel the tension that had built up in the hall purely as a result of their aggression. The policemen giving out the flowers soon began to enjoy it and pretty soon they were no different than the kids in the audience. There is no doubt that the economics student from Dartford would have made a wonderful diplomat if his career as a singer had not worked out. I was extremely glad to leave Germany a few days later, and I have to say I have no intention of returning.

WITH STEPHEN WYMAN ONSTAGE DURING
SOUNDCHECK FOR THE STONES'
CONCERT IN ATHENS, 1967.

. . .

The last concert of the tour was in Athens on April 18. It was sold out and took place in a rather grubby football stadium. The stage had been set up at one end of the pitch a long distance from the audience. It certainly was not an intimate atmosphere. In fact, there seemed to be a very strange atmosphere in Athens altogether. However, the stands were packed and the band did a fantastic job of overcoming the distance between them and the audience. Mick working harder than ever to give them a night to remember. Which, as it turned out, they certainly got.

The show was going really well and the audience was having a ball until it came to the point where Mick would normally throw the basket of flowers into the crowd. As they were at least sixty yards away, he passed the basket to Tom Keylock, who was standing in the wings, and told him to run across the football field and throw the flowers into the audience for him.

I was standing on the pitch just in front of the stage on my own. I watched as Tom jumped from the stage and ran past me toward an increasingly excited audience. Out of nowhere came two cops who rugby-tackled Tom, bringing him to the ground with a massive thump, and started to drag him off, the wind knocked out of him and his broken glasses splayed halfway round his face.

I instinctively ran toward him to try and peel the cops off but got no more than a couple of paces before I fell to the same fate. Two policemen, one with his pistol drawn, picked me up and carried me toward the huge wooden gates on the perimeter of the stadium. Before I knew it, they were opened and I was deposited unceremoniously into the street. The gates slamming shut behind me. All hell let loose in the stadium. The crowd went berserk and began to riot when they saw what the police were up to. Apparently, while Tom and I were being removed, the officer in charge mounted the stage and demanded that the power be turned off and the concert stopped. Keith, seeing Tom Keylock flattened, and having his amp die on him in mid-groove, apparently took his guitar and set about the guy with it. How he got away with it, I will never know. Meanwhile, I was left standing outside in a deserted street, thinking, *Blimey, that was a bit over-the-top*, while trying to get my bearings and remember the name of the hotel so I could get a cab back to the safety of my room.

Bill Wyman and I had decided that, as the gig in Athens was the last of the tour, we would stay on for a week's holiday. I was awakened the following morning by a phone call from Tony Calder at Immediate Records telling me that I had to return to London at once, as the Small Faces had studio time booked at Olympic Studios that evening and there was no way they could move the session. I rang Bill in his room and apologized for my sudden departure and, wishing him a pleasant holiday, left for the airport.

While waiting in a queue to go through passport control, a small man in a suit and open-necked shirt standing behind me asked if I had enjoyed my time in Athens, to which I replied, "Not particularly." He then asked if I had any money on me. I replied that it was none of his business. He then informed me that in fact it was his business, as he worked for the Greek Customs and Excise, and asked me to follow him. Whereupon I was escorted to the office of his chief to be interrogated.

I was invited to take a seat in a chair opposite an elderly, somewhat disheveled man, who sat behind a large desk in a room that looked like it hadn't seen a cleaner for some years. He began quite pleasantly, asking how long I had been in Athens and about the purpose of my very quick visit, the answers to which he already knew.

He then turned to the question of money. It seemed that the Stones, minus Bill, had left on an earlier flight and had been searched unsuccessfully for the proceeds of the previous night's concert. The Greek government was anxious to prevent the substantial fee that the Stones had received from leaving the country. He was quite convinced that I was a member of the band and that I must be carrying the dosh. Fortunately for me, I had a stack of 8 x 10 photos of the band in my briefcase, so, by pointing to each one in turn, I was able to convince him that I was not one of them. They searched me and my luggage and reluctantly sent me on my way to London. I later found out that it had been arranged for a straight guy in a suit and tie from the band's agent's office in London to fly in on the night of the concert, collect the money, and leave on the first flight out that day, having changed the drachmas into U.S. dollars on the black market.

I got back to London, went straight to the studio and did the session with the Small Faces, finishing in the early hours. I woke up the next morning and turned on the radio to get the news, only to discover that there had been a coup d'état in Greece. The army was out in force with tanks on the streets and a twenty-four-hour curfew. Poor old Bill was locked in his hotel for a week with his son Stephen and his girlfriend Astrid, and never got his well-earned holiday. While I'd had a lucky escape back to London to an all-night session with Small Faces. No wonder there had been a strange atmosphere in Athens the day before it all kicked off.

1967 was quite manic. Before I went on the Stones tour I did sessions for an album with Chris Farlowe, Vashti, Del Shannon, the Stones, and Small Faces. I got to record a massive hit, "Friday on My Mind," with The Easybeats, a hugely successful band from Australia,

MARIANNE FAITHFULL SESSION AT DECCA STUDIOS,
HAMPSTEAD. HAVING A DISCUSSION WITH MICK JAGGER
AND THE ARRANGER, ARTHUR GREENSLADE.

WITH MICK AND PAUL
MCCARTNEY AT THE
MARIANNE FAITHFULL
SESSIONS. THE SECOND
GUY ON THE RIGHT IN
THE FIRST PICTURE IS
TERRY JOHNSON.

with Shel Talmy producing. Then it was straight in with Brian Jones, who had been asked to do the music for a German murder movie called *Mord und Totschlag* that his ex-girlfriend Anita Pallenberg was starring in.

While waiting for everyone to assemble in one of the many featureless hotel lobbies on the road in England, Brian came and sat next to me and struck up a conversation. This in itself was a rare thing, as he and I had never really got on. He had agreed to write the music for the film and, having never done it before, was feeling insecure. So he was forced to try and bury the hatchet with me, as evidently I was the only person he felt could help him through the process. After a lengthy conversation, where we were both quite honest and got a lot said, I ended up feeling quite sorry for him, and knowing that he definitely had the ability to pull it off, agreed to help him out. I don't remember much about the sessions other than we got Jimmy Page to come and play some amazing guitar during the murder scene and that the German director was thrilled with the end result. After the Stones tour and the session with the Small Faces, it was straight off to the Cannes Film Festival for the premiere of Brian's movie, then back to London for more sessions with The Easybeats, Jon Mark, Del Shannon, Johnny Hallyday, The Nice, P. P. Arnold, Marianne Faithfull, The Move, The Fortunes, more Small Faces, and many all-nighters with the Stones, a couple of trips to Madrid and one to New York, and somehow I still found the time to get married.

Children of the Future,
Part One, 1968

While on a trip to California in January 1997, I returned to the Fillmore in San Francisco for the first time in thirty years. I was there to see my son Ethan playing with Brendan Benson, an artist he produced, who was opening for Tom Petty. On arrival, I was taken by my pal Mick Brigden, who ran Bill Graham Management, straight to a box in the balcony. As I looked down on the auditorium it brought back a flood of memories. Standing watching Joe Cocker and the Grease Band and feeling a hand on my shoulder, turning round to see a small figure with fuzzy hair, spectacles, and the warmest smile. "Hi, I'm Jerry Garcia, I just wanted to come over and shake your hand." What a compliment!

The first time I went there was to see the Steve Miller Band perform in 1968. After the gig, Steve took me over to meet the infamous Bill Graham, the proprietor and the most famous promoter of rock and roll in America. He was sitting at a table in the bar, in the cold neon light that makes everyone want to leave after a show. He was in a very bad mood, and being singularly unimpressed by the introduction, made it quite clear that he was in no mood for polite conversation. I took an instant dislike to him and this impression was to remain with me for many years, until I met him under completely different circumstances and came to realize what an exceptional man he was. If you want a great read you should get his book, written with Robert Greenfield, called *Bill Graham Presents*. It is a fascinating autobiography of an extraordinary man.

In March of that year I got my first break as a producer. Steve Miller came to England with his band to make his debut album, *Children of the Future*, for Capitol Records.

A few weeks earlier I had received a call from a Harvey Kornspan of San Francisco. He said that he managed the Steve Miller Band, who were completely unknown at that time. He described the band as being heavily influenced by Chicago blues and had just signed them to Capitol with supposedly the biggest deal ever done by any label. It was their intention to come to England on the *QE2* and record their album at Olympic Studios with me as the engineer and Steve Miller producing. Harvey sounded like a really nice guy but the most unlikely manager, and although it all sounded a bit hippy-dippy to me, he convinced me to accept the booking.

They duly arrived, and what an odd, somewhat disheveled assortment of road crew, musicians, girlfriends, Harvey Kornspan and a pregnant wife they were. Having rented a large house in Belgravia, they all moved in, without much ado, as one big happy family.

One evening a few days later, I got a call from the pregnant wife from, of all places, the Chelsea police station. She was in a terrible state. They had all been arrested and were to appear in magistrates' court the following morning, charged with importing drugs and possession of a dangerous firearm, and could I present myself at the court at 9:30 sharp to both guarantee their good character and, more importantly, stand bail while the great and good Harvey Kornspan sorted the whole messy business out. I began to wonder what I had got myself involved with. A bunch of drug-taking, armed American hippies?

If I went the following morning, it would be much against my own better judgment. Did I really want to be seen associating with these people, let alone stand up in court and vouch for their good characters? Suppose it got in the press. What would my mother think? When I showed some reticence, she pleaded with me, saying I was the only person they knew in the country. When that didn't do the trick, she said that she did not know what the stress of another night in a cell might do to her condition, adding that they were innocent and the whole matter could be explained.

I turned up in court the following morning in my best suit and accent. I spoke up for the even more disheveled and wretched (after a night in Chelsea nick) group, and was required by the court to stand surety for their good behavior for the remainder of their stay in the United Kingdom.

It transpired that a friend of the band in America had taken pity on them and, imagining that drugs would not be available in London, took it upon himself to send a large fruitcake through the mail, the middle of which had been stuffed full of hash. Her Majesty's Customs and Excise discovered the drugs at the port of entry and allowed the cake to be delivered by mail as normal, alerting the local police who raided the house within minutes of its arrival. During their search of the premises they discovered a flare pistol, hanging as decoration on the wall in one of the rooms. It belonged to the owner of the house and, if I remember, did not even work. But the good old English bobby, determined to make the situation look as bad as possible for these undesirables, foolishly accused them of owning a dangerous firearm. As to the drugs charges, they too were dropped when it was pointed out that it could not be proved the band had any way of knowing what was inside a parcel that had been sent by a third party.

After this, we all became the best of friends. I felt sorry for them, for the experience they'd had, and they in turn were extremely grateful to me for helping to get them out of jail. It was certainly the strangest start to a working relationship. Boz Scaggs, Lonnie Turner, Tim Davis, and I were to remain extremely close friends for many years after we had stopped working with Steve Miller, and my first impression of Harvey was borne out. He was nothing but polite and supportive to me during the entire time I knew him.

After one month of the allotted six weeks recording, we had absolutely nothing worth keeping on tape. Steve had spent the entire time experimenting with different ideas of songs, arrangements, and recording techniques, all without success. It became obvious to me that he was no ordinary musician and that he was after something very different, but was in danger of losing the trust and respect of the band as well as the services of his engineer if something did not change fairly quickly. So I sat him down and explained very nicely that I could see little point in continuing the sessions for the remaining two weeks, and unless something changed I was going to quit. He asked me what I thought was wrong and I told him that he needed a producer, as no one seemed to be in charge or was prepared to make any decisions and that the project had the demeanor of a headless chicken. He accepted what I had to say most graciously and asked if I would be prepared to stay on if I were to become the producer.

At last. Finally someone had actually asked me to produce. It was like being let out of a cage. It was unheard of for an engineer to go on to produce. The two professions were viewed as being totally separate. This was a clearly defined class system that I had long felt should be broken down.

I was twenty-six years old and had spent the previous eight years working with some great, and one or two not so great, producers, in an era that never even considered the idea of an engineer producing. Knowing that I was contributing to the production in varying degrees on some of the sessions, without the credit or remuneration, did not trouble me one bit. Perhaps I felt that I would get my chance sooner or later. I got to work with some amazing people. It was a great apprenticeship and I have never regretted a second of it.

We made the record in the remaining two weeks. Steve and the band were fantastic and responded very positively to the new regime. They were the perfect artist for my first production, being willing to try absolutely anything with great enthusiasm. I think Steve was quite relieved to lose the responsibility of producing and immediately benefitted from just being the artist and bandleader. As for me, I had a blast. Trying out ideas I had stored away over the years that had seemed too outrageous or ridiculous for the artists and producers I had been working for. I used sound effects for the first time, digging out stuff I had recorded as a junior at IBC. I would be sent out with a portable Nagra tape recorder on dead days at the studio and told to record sound effects for the library. I found a recording I had done on the Bakerloo line of a journey on the Tube I'd recorded as an excuse to get home early one day. If you listen, you can hear the platform attendant shouting "Mind the doors!" as they rumble shut and the train pulls out of the Oxford Circus station. I have no idea now why I used this effect as it seems to have no relevance to the track, but then neither does the title, "The Beauty of

Time Is That It's Snowing (Psychedelic B.B.)." I suspect I was just trying to "outweird" Steve.

This record was the first and only time I used a stereo cross-fade. The incoming track starting on the right and pushing the outgoing track off to the left as it faded in. I've tried it a couple of times since but have never been able to get it to work as effectively.

Much to my relief, Steve, the band, the wives and girlfriends, Capitol Records, and even Harvey Kornspan were all very pleased with the end result, as was I and a few hundred thousand others.

Brian Jones and the Gnawa, 1968

1968 started out with a flurry of an extraordinary mixture of artists. Working six-day weeks very often with two artists a day, starting with Peter, Paul and Mary one day, the Small Faces the next. The odd jingle for Mike Sammes, a few days with the French star Johnny Hallyday, more all-nighters with the Small Faces, then sessions with Joe Cocker, Procol Harum, Georgie Fame, and the Steve Miller Band, and a live album at the Marquee Club with The Move.

In March, with the completion of *Children of the Future* behind me, Brian Jones asked me to go to Morocco with him to record a tribe from the Atlas Mountains, the Gnawa, who were to be found playing in the market square in Marrakech at that time of the year.

He was friends with Paul Getty, Jr., who had the most wonderful palace right in the middle of the city, where we were invited to stay. Although I had reservations about my relationship with Brian, I decided to throw caution to the wind and, having never been outside

Europe, decided to take the opportunity to go on what could be an intriguing adventure.

The Gnawa were a group of about fifteen male musicians ranging from a young teenager right up to an elderly man who was their leader and led the call-and-answer chants that they all sang while creating the most complex percussive rhythms. Two of the older men played large drums hung from straps over their shoulders, beating them with long, curved sticks, while the rest played large metal castanets. They all dressed in identical white kaftans, creating music, and I am sure a message, with just harmony singing and percussion. Brian's idea was to record the rhythms and chants of this tribe and then go to New York and overdub black American blues and soul musicians on top. Thereby combining the old and the new influences of African music.

We flew to Rabat and were met there by a toothless man with an ancient Cadillac limousine that had definitely seen better days, having most recently been used to keep chickens in, and were driven to Marrakech, where we were met with the spectacle of a national festival of some sort. Tribes had assembled from the desert and were camped in carpeted tents just outside the walls of the city where they proceeded to stage camel races and mock battles on horseback. Charging at each other at full gallop. Quite a sight to perceive.

Paul and his beautiful wife Talitha greeted us, soon making me feel at ease in what could have been a rather awkward situation. I had never met either of them before and therefore was an unknown quantity as a houseguest.

I shall always remember waking up on my first morning to the sun streaming in through a beautiful stained-glass window set high in the wall, just under the ceiling some twenty feet above me. The bed was set into an alcove and was covered with fur throws and silk cushions of every hue. This was the height of luxury. I got up, showered, and went outside to be ushered by a member of staff to a stunning walled courtyard with a sunken garden in the center. There, a table had been laid and I was served breakfast with fresh orange juice from the trees in front of me. It is funny how you remember such small details, but memories so often relate to taste and smell. This was the first time I had ever eaten fresh oranges, having lived in England all my life. I had no idea that there was even a difference.

Brian had somehow managed to score as soon as we arrived and spent the entire time that we were there stoned out of his box. So I took my tape recorder into the square and got on with the job of recording the Gnawa and the amazing assortment of musicians performing there, all with the most extraordinary homemade instruments. One man sat cross-legged on the ground, singing and playing a three-stringed instrument made from a wooden cigar box that had a short pole attached to it with a small metal feather stuck on the top that vibrated every time he struck a string, creating his own percussion. Another guy played a brake drum with a rusty wrench. There were snake charmers, magicians, jugglers, and acrobats all performing in the square, interspersed with musicians in small groups or solo. Not one played any instrument that I recognized. This made for the most extraordinary cacophony of sight and sound.

Brian did not accompany me on any of my sojourns into the town. He was just stoned the whole time, so I had a blast, exploring the place on my own. Talitha very kindly took me to the market one morning to help me pick out a kaftan for my wife. She and Paul could not have been more hospitable.

Paul decided that we should invite the Gnawa to dinner and get them to perform for us in the banqueting hall of the palace. This was a vast room with archways around the perimeter framing rectangular seating areas littered with furs and multicolored cushions and a table in the middle. The walls and ceiling were covered with the most exquisite wooden marquetry. The whole experience was like something out of a movie. The Gnawa said they would be more comfortable eating outside in the courtyard, and having done so joined us inside and gave us an inspired performance that I was able to record without the superfluous noise that had been present in the market square. It was an evening I shall never forget.

The following morning I was due to return to London for a session, leaving Brian to his own devices in Marrakech. As I was preparing to leave, Paul came to my room and politely asked if I could get Brian off the premises and back to London with me. I could see that he was trying to contain his fury as he explained that Brian had somehow managed to break the telephone in his room. It had taken some months to get it installed and was almost certainly going to take the same amount of time to get it repaired. I explained that I was not Brian's keeper but would do what I could, going straight to Brian's room, waking him, and informing him in no uncertain terms that he was no longer welcome and we should leave immediately. Fortunately he was compliant and we left for London that morning. Brian with his tail between his legs, full of apologies, and me somewhat embarrassed by association. The trip did nothing for my already strained relationship with him, but was a wonderful experience on every other level.

I don't think Brian ever used what I had recorded. I know that he did return to the Atlas Mountains to record, but I don't think he ever attempted his idea of mixing the results with African American musicians.

I arrived back in London and went straight to Olympic for a Procol Harum session till three a.m. No peace for the wicked. The following weeks were taken up with the Small Faces' *Ogdens' Nut Gone Flake*, the only album that I know of that was released in a circular cover. Then the wonderful *Pentangle* album with Terry Cox, Bert Jansch, Jacqui McShee, John Renbourn and Danny Thompson, produced by Shel Talmy; *Shine on Brightly* with Procol Harum and The Move's first album for Denny Cordell; the Stones; and a Family album, produced by John Gilbert, the son of Lewis Gilbert, who was the director of most of the early Bond movies.

Then, at the end of April, came my first trip to California.

California, 1968

In the spring of 1968, Shel Talmy needed to make a trip to America. As he was almost legally blind, he found it difficult to travel alone, so he asked me to accompany him. This turned out to be another turning point in my career, as he quietly introduced me to the music business in the U.S. I was really naive, and although I had been to New York for a few days working with the Stones, I had no real experience in America at all.

We flew to New York, where Shel's lawyer, Marty Machat, offered to represent me in the States. Marty and his partner Eric Kronfeld proved to be very helpful when I started doing business there shortly thereafter, as I didn't have a clue and had previously never needed legal representation. Once again I was indebted to Shel for the introduction. My impression of New York as we left for Los Angeles a few days later was that, although architecturally breathtaking, it was full of the rudest people I had ever come across. And I was quite glad to get out of there.

Shel had booked us into the Beverly Hills Hotel and rented a black convertible Cadillac with a white interior. Sounds revolting now but back then it was the epitome of the luxurious Californian lifestyle I'd seen in movies. I could not believe my luck. What a grand way to arrive on your first trip to L.A. The first thing I noticed getting out of the car at the hotel was that wonderful sweet smell in the air that has become synonymous for me with Los Angeles. Strange, really, because in those days Los Angeles had the most massive problem with pollution, which you'd think would supersede any pleasant scent in the air.

Having checked in, Shel said he was going to get an early night, so I jumped in the car, put the roof down, asked the doorman which way was west, and drove along Sunset for my first view of the Pacific Ocean, taking in the somewhat obscene display of wealth represented in the houses on either side of the road.

On the way back, I called to see the screenwriter Robert Towne. I had met him in Madrid in 1967. He had just finished shooting *Bonnie and Clyde* and had taken himself off to Europe for a vacation. He was unlike any American I had met. Immaculately dressed, softly spoken, and quite the sophisticated gentleman. You would never imagine that he had anything to do with Hollywood and its excesses.

A few weeks after we had met, he came to London and rented a small house in a mews in Mayfair. I enjoyed his company and found him most interesting, as he was involved in a business I knew very little about. He in turn seemed fascinated by what I was doing and who I was doing it with. So, having become firm friends, I was under strict instructions to contact him on my arrival in L.A.

He was living in a California ranch–style house up in the hills behind the hotel on the top of Benedict Canyon with spectacular views of the city to the south and the valley to the north. The house was comfortable and uncomplicated, having a typical relaxed bachelor feel to it. I imagined it being a fabulous secluded environment for him to write in.

The next few days were spent accompanying Shel to meetings with various record companies around town where I got to meet most of the guys who were running the music business on the West Coast. The introductions he made gave me a whole new insight to the music business and opened the door to my future in America, where I was welcomed with open arms.

Whenever I returned to Los Angeles over the next couple of years, Robert would take me to the cool restaurants and clubs in Beverly Hills, introducing me to his friends and associates from the movie business as we went. All very heady stuff for a twenty-six-year-old from Epsom. He took me to dinner with the genius director Arthur Penn and his lovely wife, Peggy. What an unassuming, charming man he turned out to be, and one Sunday morning Robert invited me to go with him to the regular weekly drinks party at Roman Polanski's house. He and his stunningly beautiful and extremely pregnant wife, Sharon Tate, could not have been more hospitable, making me feel most welcome. It was with some horror that six weeks later I read she had been brutally murdered along with four friends by Charles Manson at that same house in Benedict Canyon.

Sailor, 1968

The night before I returned to L.A. in June, Steve Miller rang to say that he had decided to change the name of the band to Sailor and that he wanted the record to be a concept album reflecting the new name. I don't know if *Sgt. Pepper* had any influence on this decision or not but I somehow think it might have done. This was a little disconcerting, as we were to start recording in a few days and this was the first I had heard of the idea.

It was not for me to take issue with an artist that wanted to change the name of his band or make a concept album, for that matter. My job was to help him achieve whatever he wanted, within reason. I was sure that when we got together the following day in L.A. all would make sense. We met in my hotel room and Steve arrived with a large roll of paper that he ceremoniously spread across the bed. He took a pencil and began drawing wavy lines along the length of the paper, explaining that this was his visual interpretation of what he wanted the album to be. I realized I was in trouble. I had become fond of Steve, and we had developed a really good working relationship. Thinking that I was at fault for not understanding, I changed the subject and told him of an idea that I'd had on the plane on the way over, which was to start the album with an instrumental with sound effects that could, with some considerable stretch of the imagination, suggest the returning to home port of a sailor. The songs that followed could reflect the changes, both political and romantic, that he discovers as he arrives home after being away at sea for some years.

Steve and the band liked the idea, and we started recording the next day. We went down to the San Francisco docks in the middle of a foggy night to record the eerie sound of the foghorn in the harbor that begins the album. Then I set about creating a soundscape to introduce the first track. I recorded all the guys in the band singing one note mixed with an organ, took that and sped it up and slowed it down to alter the pitch and create the notes that made up the first chord of the opening track, introducing them one by one until the chord was complete. Out of that came the instrumental, "Song for Our Ancestors," which was written by Steve but played by Boz Scaggs. Sadly, this was to be the last album Boz would make with the Steve Miller Band, but fortunately he and I had become pals and I got to work with him on a couple of his solo albums for CBS, *Moments* and *Boz Scaggs & Band*.

Back in L.A., we moved into Wally Heider's studio in Hollywood and cut "Living in the U.S.A.," adding the sound of a dragster taking off from the line at the beginning and end of the song. The ballad "Dear Mary" shows Steve's voice off to perfection. He loved to stack his voice in harmony with himself. I suspect the influence of Les Paul in there somewhere, as Les had been something of a mentor in

Steve's formative years. Steve was the first singer I had worked with to do this. He managed to achieve the most extraordinary blend with himself and I have never found anyone else to use this method so effectively.

When we had finished the record, it certainly did not retain the original concept. There was no story—that had been forgotten halfway through the sessions—and the band did not change its name. That idea was never mentioned again. No matter. It worked anyway. The record is still considered to be one of his best. Many people over the years have asked me what drug I was on when constructing the opening sequence. This only goes to show what an extraordinary misguided idea so many people have with regard to the effects of drugs on popular music, as most find it incomprehensible to believe that I was completely straight and in fact have never taken drugs of any sort. Other than the odd aspirin.

Led Zeppelin,
October 1968

J immy Page and I had lost touch with each other since he had joined The Yardbirds, so you can imagine my surprise when I got a call from him out of the blue to tell me that he had put a band together with our mutual friend John Paul Jones, and a drummer and singer I had never heard of. He explained that they had assembled enough material and it was their intention to make an album, hopefully with me.

I was up for it, as Jimmy and I grew up in the same town and had been pals since the early sixties, and John had been the number-one session bass player in London for years. When I was an engineer I would see him almost every day, and a nicer guy you could not wish to meet.

Knowing that anything these two had put together was bound to be pretty good, I turned up at Olympic a couple of weeks later, not having any real idea of what I was walking into. I was blown off my feet. The album that we made in the next nine days was a landmark in rock and roll history, taking it to another level altogether.

The sound they created, the arrangements they came up with, and the standard of musicianship were equally astonishing. Each session seemed to be more exciting than the last, as what they had prepared unraveled in front of me. All I had to do was press record, sit back, and try to contain the excitement of being in the same room with what was going on.

The stereo mix of this record is certainly one of the best sounding that I ever made, but the credit has to go to the band, as all I did was try to faithfully put down on tape what they were giving me, adding a little echo here and there to enhance the mood.

We were putting together *The Rolling Stones Rock and Roll Circus* just as the album was finished. So I took my acetate to a production meeting and played it to Mick, suggesting that I felt that the band was going to be huge and therefore we should have them on the show as it would be an enormous coup. My suggestion fell on deaf ears, as Mick did not get it at all. A couple of months later I dragged George Harrison to Olympic on the way home from a Beatles session and played him the master tape with the same result, he didn't get it either. I found this slightly disconcerting as I could not understand why they did not get what was so exciting to me. Prior to this I had always felt that we all shared pretty much the same taste in music. Jimmy and John Paul Jones were from the same era with the same influences and yet Mick and George openly disliked what they had done, seeing no value in it at all. In any event, they were perfectly entitled to their opinion, and fortunately a large portion of the record-buying population disagreed with them.

. . .

It was on these sessions that I stumbled across my technique for recording stereo drums. It was a complete accident. I usually use three or four mics on drums. One over the top, one on the floor tom-tom, one on the bass drum, and one on the snare, which I very rarely use. Because we were always limited to the number of tracks available back in those days, drums would always be recorded on one track, and depending on the session, sometimes with the bass mixed with them.

We had finished a basic track and had decided to overdub an acoustic guitar on it. I took one of the Neumann U67s that I had been using on the drums to use on the guitar, and having finished the overdub, I put it back on the drums in order to start the next basic track. When I lifted the faders to listen to the drums, I found that I had inadvertently left the mic assigned to the track I had been using for the overdub, which I had placed to the far left of the stereo. As the other drum mic was in the middle, it spread the sound to the left. So I wondered what would happen if I put them left and right, and made the small adjustment of pointing the floor tom-tom mic at the snare, making the two mics equidistant from it. The result sounded enormous, with the completely different perspective that stereo brings. It is completely unnatural to have the drums spread across the entire stereo picture, so I panned each track to half left and half right, ending up with the technique I have used ever since. There is no question that if I had not been working with John Bonham and the extraordinary sound he was giving me, I would not have spotted it. A prerequisite to this working is that you must have a drummer who gives you a good sound in the first place, as well as a pair of Neuman U67s or 47s, or Telefunken 251s.

There are all kinds of representations of this method on You-Tube, claiming to be my version. None of these are really accurate. Contrary to popular belief, I have never used a tape measure. It is not that precise, it is just a matter of using common sense and believing it will work, making small adjustments depending on the kit, the balance the drummer is giving you, and what he is playing.

MY DRUM MIKE
TECHNIQUE, AS USED
WITH JEREMY STACEY
ON THE BENMONT TENCH
ALBUM *YOU SHOULD BE
SO LUCKY* AT SUNSET SOUND
STUDIOS IN LOS ANGELES.

The Beatles, 1969

In December of 1968, while sitting at home on a night off, I answered the telephone to a man with a Liverpudlian accent claiming to be Paul McCartney. I thought it was Mick Jagger trying to be amusing, so I told him to stop messing about and asked him what he wanted. The man persisted, and much to my shock and embarrassment, it really was Paul McCartney.

He told me that he had an idea for the band to write all new material and then record it live in front of an audience for a TV show and for release as an album. The venue was to be discussed, but it would be somewhere exotic. He then asked if I would be interested in making the record with them. I felt like I'd won the lottery. He told me that they were all to meet at a soundstage at Twickenham Film Studios on January 2nd, 1969, when they were to start rehearsals, and asked if I could be there.

BEATLES SETUP AT TWICKENHAM FILM STUDIOS. PAUL,
GEORGE, RINGO, MAL EVANS, YOKO, JOHN, AND ME.

I turned up on the appointed day with enormous anticipation. After all, they were the biggest band in the world and were at the height of their career. I had worked with many successful artists but I have to say, this was quite different. I have always loved vocal harmony and had constantly been blown away by the extraordinary sound that the blend of John, Paul, and George achieved. Add to that their songwriting and their reinvention of recorded sound, and you can imagine how I felt as I walked through the enormous doors of the soundstage at Twickenham that morning.

Mal Evans, the band's trusty road manager, was there to greet me with a huge smile as I arrived. He and his young assistant, Kevin, made me feel most welcome. The soundstage was huge, far bigger than was necessary for what we had to do. We set the band up with Ringo on a rostrum at one end facing down the room, with the other three sitting facing him. A small PA with three vocal mics was added, and we were ready to go.

They had enlisted the services of Michael Lindsay-Hogg, a charming and brilliant director, to shoot a documentary of the making of the TV show and album. He and I had just finished working together on *The Rolling Stones Rock and Roll Circus* so we knew each other well and got on just great. Each of us taking comfort in the presence of the other, being the new boys on the block. There was a small film crew with two or three cameras and a sound guy with a couple of mics on booms to record the sound for the film.

The band showed up in dribs and drabs—Paul first, Ringo second, followed by George and then John and Yoko. They were reconvening, having not seen one another for a while, so the usual social repartee took place as we all slowly acclimatized and eventually got round to discussing in more detail what we were about to embark on. The only slightly strange thing to me was that instead of politely melting into the background as they started to work, Yoko remained sitting on the same chair as John, sometimes answering for him when he was addressed by one of the others. He seemed quite happy with this, so everyone realizing that this was to be the way of things, proceeded as best they could. I had never witnessed anything quite like it and felt very uncomfortable, so heaven knows how the others felt. It was almost like having a fifth member in the band all of a sudden.

After they had finally run through the first song a couple of times, Paul turned to me and asked what I thought they should do for an intro. I nearly fell over in shock. I thought I had been employed to just engineer and here I am in the first hour of rehearsals being asked for my input into the arrangement. I responded as quickly and confidently as I could and suggested a way of playing the intro, which they liked, and we were off. I was amazed at how quickly and easily I was accepted, each guy individually making an attempt to put me at ease and make me feel part of the team. It was only then that I realized that George Martin was not to be involved. I assumed that was because it was a live recording and did not require the normal studio production associated with their records. In the book *Recording The Beatles*, it is suggested that the reason I got the job was that I had a union card to enable me to work on a movie. Like so much of the info in that book regarding my involvement with the band, this is complete nonsense, as I have never belonged to any union other than the musicians' and as I had nothing to do with the film sound it would not have been necessary anyway.

Whenever we took a break we would continue to discuss the how, where, and why of the show. Paul had the idea to take a cruise ship full of Beatles fans to an ancient open-air amphitheater somewhere in Tunisia and put the show on there. This did not go down terribly well with the others, particularly Ringo, whose main concern seemed to be what the food would be like.

On the second day, things came to a head among the band. The entire crew left the room in great haste to allow them some privacy to sort out their differences.

I have often thought that being in a band can be likened to being in a marriage. Members spend their lives cooped up with one another for weeks on end, sharing some very strange and sometimes extremely boring times together, magnifying the differences between the personalities that are bound to exist between any group of humans, that have nothing to do with the creative mix that they share as a unit.

Equally, there invariably comes a time when one or another in a band becomes frustrated with the status quo and wants to take a different musical path and set sail on his own.

I have a very clear memory of sitting outside in the bleak surroundings of the soundstage at Twickenham on that cold gray afternoon with Denis, the line producer for the film, both of us praying that the elation of being employed for a project with the most successful artist in the world was not about to come to a grinding halt after only two days.

It is not my place to discuss any detail of what happened, but it is common knowledge that George left the band and was persuaded to return a couple of days later.

Once that was over and done with we carried on and it seemed that all was quickly forgotten. The only visible change was that although Yoko still came to the studio most days she no longer occupied John's chair with him. This could well have been a coincidence as she did occupy herself in other ways. She would have a driver come to the studio every day with a folder containing any press clipping that mentioned her or the band, taken from publications all over the world. One such day a guy turned up with an envelope containing the photographs that Ethan Russell had taken at the *Rolling Stones Rock and Roll Circus* TV show. John brought them over to show me and Michael Lindsay-Hogg, as we had both worked on it, and suggested that Ethan be asked to join us as the stills photographer for the duration of the project. This was great news for me as this meant that I would have another pal on the team.

John had recently appeared in the Stones' *Rock and Roll Circus* in a supergroup that was an unlikely combination of him, Keith Richards, Eric Clapton, and Mitch Mitchell. It was unrehearsed, and the performance was just a bit of fun really.

I was in my booth, way up in the gods, recording the sound for the show, and the area on the set where they were playing was obscured from my view. All was going well until I heard this extraordinary noise that sounded like someone stepping on the cat. I panicked, thinking that a piece of equipment might be malfunctioning, while peering at the screen trying to see if it was adversely affecting the guys onstage. All of a sudden a picture appeared of a small figure with a black bag over its head with a mic cable disappearing into it. It turned out to be Yoko, who had decided to contribute to the proceedings. How anyone could have considered her intrusion to be in any way musical is a complete mystery to me.

After a few days, the dust having settled, The Beatles got back into a normal routine of rehearsing the songs they intended to use, but it became increasingly obvious that the question of a venue for the show was not going to be resolved easily. The enthusiasm for the whole idea of going abroad began to wane when Ringo announced that he was not at all happy with the idea. So when there was no argument from John and George, it was dropped.

This created something of a problem, as Paul's original idea of a TV show had been discarded. At least there was still enthusiasm for the songs that were being rehearsed and for playing them live, but we had a half-made documentary with no end. So it was decided that we would move to Savile Row and film the band completing the process of rehearsing the songs and then get Michael to light the studio properly in order to shoot and record the band playing the songs in a live performance as if in a show.

The Beatles had commissioned a studio to be built in the basement of their office building in Savile Row and we were informed that it was ready for use. So one evening, after we had finished at Twickenham, I was taken by George Harrison to check it out.

The band had formed Apple Electronics in 1967, for the purpose of designing and building innovative consumer electronics. It was headed up by Yanni Alexis Mardas, whom Lennon had nicknamed Magic Alex and I knew as Alex the Greek. I had come across this guy before with the Stones on their 1967 tour of Europe. He turned up at a gig and sold Mick on the idea of building a light show for use on the tour, the likes of which had never been seen. Having been paid for the components, he reappeared a couple of weeks later with what could only be described as very basic disco lighting. Each guitar amp onstage had small lamps attached to it that would change color and intensity with the level and frequency of the sound it emitted. I came to the conclusion that at best he suffered from delusions and at worst he was a complete fraud. He sure could talk the talk, and a couple of years earlier had convinced The Beatles that he was an electronics genius. In fact, according to his ex-flatmate, Marianne Faithfull's first husband and art gallery owner John Dunbar, he was nothing more than a TV repairman.

Brian Jones had met Alex shortly after he arrived in England from Greece in 1965 and introduced him to John Lennon who had been impressed with his "Nothing Box," on display in Dunbar's gallery, which turned out to be exactly that, a small box with random blinking lights that John would supposedly sit and stare at while under the influence of LSD. It was at John Dunbar's gallery that he met Yoko, as she was also an exhibitor there.

Alex took me out to dinner in London a few weeks after the Stones tour had finished, to pitch me his ideas. Among many claims that he made to me that evening was that he reckoned he could build a domestic robot that would clean the house and answer the door, knowing who was friend or foe. He had convinced George that he could build the most innovative studio yet, claiming he could design and build a 72-track tape machine. At this point in time we were only up to eight tracks. The only product that I can recall to surface from Apple Electronics was a transistor radio that looked like an apple.

I turned up at Savile Row dreading what I was going to find there. Particularly as it was going to be down to me to make it work. My fears were not unfounded. It was apparent that Alex knew little or nothing about the recording process. The console looked like something out of a 1930s Buck Rogers science fiction movie. Above it on the wall were eight loudspeakers that were about the size and thickness of a large ham and cheese sandwich. I had previously hinted to George that I had little or no faith in Alex and was put very sharply in my place. So when I all but burst into laughter at what I was confronted with as I walked into the control room, he accused me of being biased, having made up my mind before even trying it out. In any event, it soon became obvious to all concerned, and much to George's chagrin, that they had been ripped off and that the whole setup was as much of a joke as I had originally assumed it would be.

George Martin came to the rescue and arranged for us to borrow equipment from Abbey Road, which was delivered and installed by the wonderful Dave Harries, who among his many accomplishments went on in later years to manage Air Studios for George Martin and build British Grove Studios for Mark Knopfler, in my opinion currently the best studio in England.

We carried on in much the same manner as we had started. I set the band up in the round with a small PA and they continued to rehearse the songs, playing and singing live. The major difference being that we were in a much cozier atmosphere than the cavernous soundstage at Twickenham and I had a proper control room with really good equipment to record what they were doing. After a couple of days, Billy Preston swung by to say hi and was immediately told to sit down at the electric piano and join in. What a bonus that turned out to be. He was an old pal of the band from their days at the Star-Club in Hamburg and they were all really pleased to see him. Apart from his genius as a musician he was great to have around and definitely contributed to the ever-improving mood of the sessions.

During those days at Savile Row, I felt increasingly privileged to witness the four most famous musicians in the world hone the songs they had written into acceptable arrangements in their simplest

form, without relying on the incredibly complex and innovative production process that they had become famous for with the making of
Sgt. Pepper. Having proved that they were the masters of the "produced" record, they had reverted right back to the beginning and
were performing live with no overdubbing or sonic effects to distract
the listener or enhance the music. There was nothing to hide behind.
So it crossed my mind that possibly it would be of interest to their
fans to have the same insight I was experiencing. Having no real end
in sight for the album, one evening after our session at Savile Row, I
took it upon myself to take the multitrack recordings I had made
during rehearsals to Olympic Studios to mix and edit what I thought
could be an idea for the album. This was to show in an audio documentary what I had witnessed in the previous days, as a "fly on the
wall" insight to the four of them interacting, having fun, jamming,
taking the mickey, stopping and starting and creating some wonderful music, warts and all. I had five acelates cut the following morning
and gave one each to the band, keeping one for myself, saying it was
just an idea and asking them to take a listen. The next day I got a resounding NO from each of them, which I completely understood and
had fully expected.

A couple of days later we were all having lunch on the third floor.
Ringo and I were in conversation about the building and its attributes and he asked me if I had ever been up on the roof, saying it
had a wonderful view of the West End of London. So he took me and
Michael Lindsay-Hogg up there, showing us a large area of flat roof
with wonderful views of the city stretching away to the southwest. I
suggested that if they wanted to play to a large crowd, why not play
on the roof to the whole of the West End. We went back downstairs
and put it to the others, and after some discussion it was agreed. As

the Savile Row police station was only a couple of hundred yards away we knew the concert would probably not last long, but the police stopping it would all be part of the fun.

I ran cables down the stairwell in the middle of the building to the control room in the basement and we were ready to go. The band were in an excellent mood and they needed to be, as it was a cold and windy winter's day.

As expected, the concert was stopped by the police after half an hour or so, but we did get a great version of "One After 909." I had not heard it before so it came as a bit of a shock. Apparently it is the first song John and Paul wrote together.

One morning before the others arrived at the studio, George asked me if I would stay behind at the end of the day to cut a demo with him of a song he had written, as he didn't want to play it in front of the others. So we waited for everyone to leave and he went out into the empty studio and played "Something in the Way She Moves," which might just be the greatest song he ever wrote. He came into the control room, and after having it played back to him, he asked what I thought of it, as he seemed unsure. I told him it was brilliant and that he must play it to the others. I can only assume that his confidence had been dented as a result of living in the shadow of John and Paul.

In the last week that we were recording at Savile Row, I came up the stairs from the basement at the end of the day, and as I turned the corner in the hallway on the ground floor I saw John Lennon opening the front door and greeting Allen Klein. I nearly fell back down the stairs with shock. Allen had bought The Rolling Stones' management from Andrew Oldham in 1967. The Stones were never happy about the arrangement, most especially when they discovered that he had acquired the rights to all their masters and publishing until 1971. I was having dinner with Klein in London one night in 1968 when he announced that he was going to get The Beatles. I told him he was bonkers, but here we were a year later, him waving hello to me with the grin of a Cheshire cat as John ushered him into the office for what may have been their first meeting.

After exactly a month, on the 31st of January, we finished at Savile Row with a proper performance of all the songs as we had discussed and went our separate ways.

Children of the Future,
Part Two

The following day I returned to California to start the Steve Miller Band's third album, *Brave New World*. We were getting on fine until I got a call from The Beatles, asking if Steve would let me go for a couple of weeks, to return home to London to do some sessions for what became *Abbey Road*. They made him an offer he could not refuse, saying they would pay all the expenses incurred by the delay to his recording schedule. So the band got to hang out in a hotel in L.A. courtesy of The Beatles, while I disappeared back to London for what proved to be a somewhat grueling few days.

I went straight from the plane to Apple for a couple of days, and then to Olympic Studios for an all-night session with the Stones till six a.m. Then to Apple again in the afternoon before going on to the Albert Hall that evening to record Jimi Hendrix in concert.

This was a complete disaster. The Albert Hall was originally designed for classical music and not in any way for loud rock and roll. I had recorded The Rolling Stones there a few years earlier but that was in the days when you could not hear a note of music for the wall of screaming teenage girls, and the amplifiers were considerably smaller, therefore not nearly as loud, so the acoustics were not so much of an issue. The acoustics have been improved dramatically in recent years but in 1969 it may have been the worst venue in the UK for Hendrix to play. It sounded like an enormous indoor swimming pool.

I spoke to Jimi after the soundcheck, suggesting **that if** he wanted anyone in the audience to hear a single note of **what he** played that he and Noel Redding, the bass player, should use much smaller amps and for them to play at a much quieter level than they were used to. I knew I was wasting my time, but I also knew that the recording would be useless if he did not make some kind of compromise.

He was charming and said he understood the problem and would consider what I had said. When the show began, as I expected, he completely ignored my suggestion. If anything, he turned up and the net result was an unusable cacophony of sound.

I was set up in a dressing room backstage, and as soon as I realized how bad it was I decided not to waste my time, and having told the assistant engineer to change reels when necessary, I went home.

The following morning I got an extremely irate call from Mike Jeffery, Jimi's manager, asking where the hell I was when they went backstage to listen to a playback after the concert. I politely told him that as Jimi had decided not to take my advice, which was entirely his prerogative, the recording was completely useless. Therefore there was little point in me sitting there all evening listening to the racket going onstage. This may well have been the last conversation I had with Mike and I was never to see Jimi again.

T he next day I went into Trident Studios in Soho to record "I Want You (She's So Heavy)" with The Beatles. The session finished at five a.m. and I went home, grabbed my things, and left for L.A. that morning, starting back in the studio with Steve and the band the next day.

A month later, we had almost finished *Brave New World* and I returned to London to spend the next few weeks working with The Beatles on material for *Abbey Road*, at both Olympic and Abbey Road, interspersed with the Stones, working on *Let It Bleed* at Olympic, and with George Harrison, producing an album with Billy Preston.

After my first week back home, Steve decided to come to London to do some mixing with me and hang out for a few days. I had a session booked at Olympic on a Sunday with the Fab Four, and I invited him to come along to meet them. Unfortunately their office had inadvertently told only Paul and Mal Evans about the session. So we found ourselves with a studio full of Beatles instruments and no band. Not to be outdone by the situation, Paul asked Steve if he had a song. Steve replied that he didn't but had an idea for one, and by five o'clock the following morning we had "My Dark Hour" finished. Paul played drums and bass and added the most powerful vocal harmony to the chorus, and Steve sang lead and played guitar. A good time was had by all and the song ended up on *Brave New World*.

Steve had plenty of time to spare on the days we were not working, while I was darting from one session to the next. So he went to Anello & Davide, the famous boot- and shoemaker on the Tottenham

Court Road, and ordered thirteen pairs of Beatle boots. They were
not ready by the time he returned to the States, as they took several
weeks to be made, and some months later I agreed to pick them up
and take them to him in San Francisco. I had arranged to stop off in
Boston on the way, to meet Phil Walden, the manager of the Allman
Brothers, to discuss the possibility of producing their first album.

My luggage was the last off the plane. I had two suitcases, one for
my clothes and the other full of Beatle boots of various hues. The
customs guy was really pissed off by the time he got to me, having
just processed a large portion of the contents of a 747. He took one
look at what stood before him and decided on a course of revenge for
the way his day had gone thus far.

I usually traveled dressed as conventionally as possible. The experience of traveling with the Stones across many borders had proven
invaluable. However, on this occasion I was wearing jeans and a
suede fringe jacket. This, coupled with the length of my hair, trig-
gered the blue revolving lights in the bastard's eyes. He opened the
case containing my clothes first, searching every item until the entire contents were spread out on his table. Finding nothing untoward
did nothing to quench his desire for a kill. He moved on to my briefcase, reading my phone book and diary from cover to cover. A regular
bloody Sherlock Holmes. I had a packet of peppermints, which were
pounced on with glee. "What have we here?" he muttered. "Peppermints," came the reply. "Please, do have one." The packet was ripped
open without ceremony and the innocent little mints had their wrap-
pers ripped off one by one. They were sniffed, licked, and inspected
from every angle. All to no avail. Then he moved on to the second
suitcase. "What's in here?" he sneered. "Boots," I replied, my heart
sinking. Now I was sure at the very least I was going to be done for

boot smuggling. "I am bringing them here for a friend in San Francisco, he had them made for him on his last trip to London . . ." I trailed off, realizing that the more I spoke, the guiltier I appeared.

Beatle boots, you may recall, have Cuban heels. This was clearly going to make his month. I was told to step back from the table while he set about Steve's boots as one possessed, checking each heel for a false trapdoor, tapping and twisting his way through all twenty-six. On finding nothing, he started the whole routine all over again from the beginning. Finally, after nearly an hour, he gave up and begrudgingly told me to pack up my belongings, which were now in a large heap on the table, and to leave, as if I had delayed him and caused him the most awful inconvenience.

Just as I lifted the last item onto my trolley I felt a tap on my shoulder. It was two plainclothesmen, who flashed their badges and asked me to accompany them to a small oblong room nearby. I have no idea if my name was on a list, by association with those I had been working and in some cases traveling with in the past or what, but these guys seemed quite convinced that I was up to no good, and it wasn't boot smuggling they were trying to pin on me.

I should reiterate that I am completely straight and have never taken drugs—hard, soft, liquid, or powder—at any time. Boring, but true. So, as you can imagine, after I'd spent the previous few years, six or seven days a week, with some of the most notorious users in the western hemisphere, my one big fear was getting busted, since I knew of more than one case of drugs being planted by the authorities so as to be sure of not having a wasted trip. Brian Jones told me that when he was busted at his flat in London the police planted hash in his sock drawer, and Pattie Boyd told me that when she was married to George Harrison the police raided their house in Esher and came out of the bedroom claiming that they had found drugs in a pair of George's shoes. Whereupon she said, "There must be some mistake, as we keep our drugs in the bowl over there," pointing to the coffee table in the middle of the room.

I was particularly concerned as I entered the room with Tweedledum and Tweedledee. They played the classic good cop/bad cop routine. One spoke softly and almost apologetically, while the other stood menacingly a few paces away, only speaking in order to reinforce the darker side of why I was in that room. The nice guy asked me if I ever smoked grass. My reply was that I did not, but even if I did, did he really think I would discuss it with him?

The unpleasant one told me to give him my jacket, took it to the other end of the room, and with his back turned to me, went as if to put his hand in the pocket. At this point I flipped, stating that I had cooperated completely for the last hour and that if he wanted to search my jacket he was very welcome to, but he had to do it in front of me where I could see what he was doing. He walked slowly back up the room, and I asked him to open his hand before putting it in my pocket. I thought for one awful moment that I had really blown it. There was a silent pause, filled with a deadly stare from the arsehole, that was broken by the good guy saying, "I don't think we need keep you any longer, Mr. Johns. I'm sorry for any inconvenience we may have caused you."

I was out of there like a rat up a pipe, I can tell you. I was amazed to find Phil Walden still waiting in a completely deserted area outside customs. "Hi, Glyn," he hollered, "welcome to America!"

WITH THE BEATLES AT SAVILE ROW.

Back to The Beatles

On the 1st of May 1969, I got a call from John and Paul asking me to meet them at Abbey Road. I walked into the control room and was confronted by a large pile of multitrack tapes. They told me that they had reconsidered my concept for the album that I had presented to them in January and had decided to let me go ahead and mix and put it together from all the recording that we had done at Savile Row. I was thrilled at the idea and asked when they would be available to start. They replied that they were quite happy for me to do it on my own as it was my idea. I left feeling elated that they would trust me to put the album together without them, but soon realized that the real reason had to be that they had lost interest in the project.

I went straight into the mix room at Olympic and spent the next three nights mixing and editing the album and, having finished, pre-

sented it to the band at the session we had at Olympic the following day.

I had been retained originally as an engineer and was quite happy
with that, even when I realized that George Martin was not producing. He did come to Twickenham a couple of times to check us out.
He had arranged for the gear to be loaned for the recording at Savile
Row and turned up on the day we did the filming on the roof, but had
nothing to do with the production of the music. At the outset I was
quite embarrassed when I realized he was not going to be involved.
A couple of days into the project I asked Paul where George Martin
was, only to be told that they had decided not to use him. By the time
we moved to Savile Row, George, realizing I was in an awkward position, was kind enough to take me to lunch in order to put my mind at
rest, saying I was doing a great job, everything was fine, and I was
not stepping on his toes in any way. What a gentleman he is.

Having delivered the mixed master of my version of *Let It Be*, I
approached each member of the band separately, asking if I could
have a production credit on the album when it was released. I made
it quite clear that I was only asking for that and not a royalty.
Paul, George, and Ringo had no objection to my request but John was
suspicious and could not understand why I was not asking for a royalty. I explained that I felt, because of their stature, the sales of the
album would not be affected by my involvement one way or another,
so a credit would be a fair settlement for what I had done, as by association it could only be positive for my career in the future. I never
got an answer from John.

As it turned out, none of this mattered, as in the end, after the
group broke up, John gave the tapes to Phil Spector, who puked all
over them, turning the album into the most syrupy load of bullshit I
have ever heard. My master tape, perhaps quite rightly, ended up on

a shelf in the tape store at EMI. At least my version of the single of "Get Back"/"Don't Let Me Down" had been released in April 1969.

Since that first meeting in late January 1969, John had been pitching the idea to the others that Allen Klein was the man to manage them. Paul wanted his father-in-law, Lee Eastman, a New York lawyer, to take over the job and was not happy about Klein at all. As I had known Allen for a couple of years, through his involvement with The Rolling Stones, Ringo and George both approached me separately for my opinion of him. My relationship with Allen was quite amenable, as he had always treated me with respect, but was irrelevant as it had no bearing on the magnitude of what they were discussing with him. So my suggestion to both of them was to talk to Mick Jagger and Keith Richards, as they had firsthand experience of the man as a manager and would be able to give a far more accurate picture of the guy than me. My advice seemed to fall on deaf ears, as they came out on John's side and agreed to the idea. This left Paul isolated from the others and the object of Klein's determination to win him over.

Klein came to London with the sole objective of closing the deal, and having had an unsuccessful meeting with Paul in the morning, he left for Heathrow to return home to New York. Paul and I were working together in Olympic that afternoon, and there was a noticeable sense of relief when he heard that Klein had left for the airport. However, Klein had second thoughts about leaving and decided to have one more attempt at changing Paul's mind face-to-face. Unannounced, Klein walked into the studio, and very quickly it became apparent that as voices were raised a private conversation was taking place. I turned off all the mics in the room and left them to it. The control room of a studio is isolated from the recording room where the musicians play, but even all that acoustic treatment was not enough to prevent me hearing Paul McCartney defend himself against Allen Klein's attempt at bullying him into submission. It was extremely unpleasant to witness.

Klein got his way and he took over management of the band. After Brian Epstein's death, they had been something of a rudderless ship and he had left them with an abysmally poor record deal with EMI. Renegotiating record deals was a forte of Allen's and I am sure he earned his commission several times over with that one stroke. He came in at a tricky time. Paul's original idea for *Let It Be* had not come to fruition, and they were left with a documentary film that was in a mess. Michael Lindsay-Hogg was a TV director of some note and was not used to using film. So he had ended up with hours and hours of footage from three or four cameras with little or no coordination or continuity kept between them. It took a year to sort it all out and for him to come up with a finished movie. We were all summoned to a viewing on the 3rd of October in the West End, when Allen Klein decided that there was too much footage involving other people and it should concentrate more on the four members of the band. So this meant that there was no interaction between The Beatles and anyone else, which, in my opinion, ruined what had been a much more interesting film, but then I *would* say that, as it was mostly footage of me that was cut.

Once the film had been reedited to Klein's specifications, John and Paul asked me to change some of the material on my version of the album. This included going in with John to redo his vocal on "Across the Universe," a track that had been recorded in 1968. This was to be my last experience working with him. He was in a very strange mood. I put him in the vocal booth in the mix room at Olympic and ran the multitrack tape to get a recording level on his voice and to let him warm up and get into what he was doing. After one run-through, I suggested that we should take it. Whereupon he went ballistic, saying that he would never sing it like that again, asking why the hell I had not taken it the first time he sang it. I explained that it would not have been possible as I needed to get a level on his voice. He begrudgingly sang it again and left in a huff. He had been around the recording process long enough to know that what he was complaining about was ridiculous, so I put it down to him being under the influence of some substance. It was a sad way to finish after what had been a really pleasant working relationship up to that point. He was hysterically funny, having the quickest wit of anyone I have ever met.

The delay in finishing the film caused *Let It Be* to be the last album released by The Beatles, although the last album they recorded together was *Abbey Road*. George Martin and Geoff Emerick were restored to their rightful roles to finish the record in grand style. Shortly after this, The Beatles finally broke up, reuniting only to sever their connection with Klein a few years later.

David Anderle,
March 1969

While in Los Angeles making *Your Saving Grace* with the Steve Miller Band, I was introduced to Lee Hazlewood and his girlfriend, Suzi Jane Hokum. Lee was enjoying success as an artist and producer, having just had a huge hit with Nancy Sinatra's "These Boots Are Made for Walkin'." Not exactly my cup of tea musically, but he was a really nice guy.

Suzi Jane took me to the Whiskey on Sunset Boulevard one night to see a band I had never heard of, Delaney & Bonnie. I thought they were great, but the guy that impressed me most that night was the piano player in the band, Leon Russell. I had never heard anyone play like that, he was like an entire rhythm section all on his own.

We ran into Suzi's friend David Anderle and joined him in a booth at the back of the room for the rest of the evening. He was running Elektra Records on the West Coast for Jac Holzman, having previously worked for Brian Wilson and the Beach Boys at their label,

Brother Records. We hit it off immediately, and that chance meeting was the beginning of a lasting friendship.

He invited me to his office the next day to see the studio that Jac had built with help from Bruce Botnick and John Haeny, two genius engineers in L.A. The studio had not been open long. Bruce had already made a Doors album there with Paul Rothchild producing, and to demonstrate the sound of the place David and John took me into the control room to play me the Delaney & Bonnie album that they had just completed. The sound was incredible. The combination of an extraordinary rhythm section, Leon Russell's piano, Bonnie's voice, and the recorded sound was like nothing I had ever heard.

David gave me a test pressing of the album, and when I returned to London I lent it to George Harrison, who was so impressed he decided that Apple Records should release it in the UK. When David and Jac heard of his intentions they had to pay a quick visit to London to explain politely that the world rights to the record belonged to Elektra. I was mixing *Let It Be* at the time and they came by Olympic to say hi as an excuse to hear the new Beatles album before anyone else. They were discreet enough not to mention the real reason for their visit to the UK, and it was only recently that David told me of George's innocent intention of piracy. George soon got over his disappointment, and some months later, having made friends with Delaney, went on the road with the band and ended up playing at Carnegie Hall with them, adding Duane Allman as a second guest. Another wonderful night of musical collaboration that was never to be repeated, and I was fortunate enough to be there.

It soon became apparent to me that David Anderle had the extraordinary gift of making anyone who was the least bit creative feel incredibly comfortable and secure, while never hiding his true feelings, positive or negative. He was certainly the least threatening and

LUNCH IN L.A., 2013. L TO R: ABE SOMER,
JERRY MOSS, ME, DAVID ANDERLE.

most uncomplicated record company executive I had ever come across. The result being that, wherever he has gone since, he has attracted wonderful talent and maintained great relationships with some of the most important artists in the business.

Jerry Moss spotted this not long after David's exit from Elektra in 1969 and offered him a home with no title at A&M, reporting only to Jerry. David's office at the old Charlie Chaplin Studios on La Brea became the hang for anyone who was anybody in the seventies. The quality and availability of the drugs there may have had some bearing on it, although I was never to witness such goings-on.

The next time I saw Elektra Studios was to record the demos for Rita Coolidge with David producing. I remember this session well, as although I had met him many times before socially, it was the first time I had recorded Jim Gordon, the much-sought-after session drummer. The list of artists he played with is like a who's who of popular music in the sixties and seventies. He was in Derek and the Dominos with Eric Clapton and cowrote their biggest hit, "Layla," with him. At this time he was playing with Delaney & Bonnie.

I went to place my normal three mics on his drums when he rudely demanded to know where the rest of the mics were. Not a good start. I explained politely that this was how I was going to record him and not to worry. This did nothing to appease his surly attitude and he demanded that I put a mic on every drum. I had a huge respect for him as a musician and had always found him to be pleasant company, so I was somewhat taken back by his attitude and I did not appreciate being told how to do my job. I just walked away, saying, "How about you play the drums and I will record them?" He seemed to approve of the drum sound when he came and heard the first playback and kept quiet for the rest of the session. He was in love with Rita at the time, and as it was unrequited, when he was not playing he spent most of the time pacing up and down in a very disturbed fashion. Sadly, many years later he was diagnosed with schizophrenia. This caused him to hear voices that told him to murder his mother, which he duly did, by attacking her with a hammer and stabbing her to death. For which he is still serving time in California.

David got Rita a deal with A&M with the demos we recorded that day and went on to produce several hits with her.

The only other time I used Elektra Studios was with the Stones, working for a couple of days on *Let It Bleed*. We went in with Leon Russell and the amazing fiddle player Byron Berline and worked on a version of "Country Honk." I remember running a microphone out onto La Brea Avenue to record a car honking its horn for the intro.

I don't remember him being there, but apparently it was Jack Nitzsche who recommended Merry Clayton to come in and sing with Mick on "Gimme Shelter," which along with "Street Fighting Man" is without question one of my favorite Stones tracks. She was called very late at night and, being heavily pregnant and already in bed, was singularly unimpressed at being disturbed at such a late hour. She had no idea who The Rolling Stones were and was reluctant to come. Her husband got on the phone and once he realized who the session was for persuaded her to change her mind. She was absolutely amazing. None of us had ever heard anything quite like what she produced that night. I practically had to stand her in another room, her voice was so powerful. She did three amazing takes, standing there with her hair still in curlers, and went home. Her husband was quite right. The performance made her very famous and quite rightly so. The tragedy was that not long after the session she had a miscarriage and lost her baby. Believing that the effort that she put into her performance that night may well have been the cause, she could never listen to the Stones' version of the song.

Let It Bleed may well be my favorite Stones album. Great songs. "Midnight Rambler," "Monkey Man," and "You Can't Always Get What You Want," with Jimmy Miller playing drums and the London Bach Choir, which is a wonderful cross-pollination of cultures. There was some discussion about which should be the A-side of the single— it was between it and "Honky Tonk Women." I wanted "You Can't Always Get What You Want" and fought quite hard for it. Mick disagreed, and when Eric Clapton visited us in the studio one evening he had me play both tracks in order for Eric to choose which he thought should be the A-side. Eric, telling me I must have a screw loose, chose "Honky Tonk Women." It went to number one both in the UK and America for several weeks and could easily be their best-known song. Just shows you what I know.

Jimmy Miller played cowbell on the basic track, and as I was alone in the control room when it was recorded, in a rare generous moment Mick told me that I had produced it. All this did was confirm to me that at that point in time neither Mick nor Keith had any real understanding of what a producer really did.

There is another story showing my total incompetence during the making of *Let It Bleed*. Jimmy Miller and I were mixing "You Got the Silver" and he had the idea of putting reverse echo on the lead guitar. This is achieved by turning the tape upside down and playing it backwards while putting echo on the guitar and recording the return from the chamber on an empty track. I had never done it before and I miscalculated which was the empty track to record on and succeeded in erasing Mick's vocal. Unfortunately, Mick was ten thousand miles away in Australia, making the movie *Ned Kelly*. I was mortified, but fortunately there was a positive result to my mistake. We asked Keith to sing it. I think I am right in saying it is his first lead vocal on a Stones album and he did a really fine job. From that moment on I always wanted to make an acoustic album with him. He was an exceptional acoustic guitar player and that instrument was the perfect vehicle for his voice.

I would always call in and see David whenever I was in L.A. More often than not staying with him and his first wife, Sherril. It was on one such a visit that he played me a demo tape of a band he had been sent that morning by his childhood pal and attorney Abe Somer. They had a really interesting sound that was a blend of country rock and American folk music all wrapped up in wonderful harmonies. As David seemed quite interested in producing them, I asked if he would consider us doing it together. He liked the idea, and we jumped on a plane to Kansas to go and meet The Ozark Mountain Daredevils.

They were a great bunch of guys and enormous fun to work with and turned out to be the most prolific writers. I remember going through more than eighty songs before starting the first album. It was David's and my second time producing together and I have to say it worked well, balancing each other out with David being the laid-back good guy and me being the considerably less patient workaholic slave driver. In the early summer of 1973, they came to Olympic studios in London to make their first album. This was great fun to record and resulted in the Top 30 hit "If You Wanna Get to Heaven."

It was decided to go to the Ozark Mountains for the second album. The band had rented an old wooden house in the middle of nowhere, the ground floor of which we used as a recording studio. It was the most surreal experience. The band had found a little old lady who lived locally to come and cook the most revolting food I have ever eaten. She was a sweetheart and meant well, but there was a cog missing when it came to preparing food. I remember the one time I ventured off the property on my own, being given strict instructions to go into only one of the two local stores that were set diagonally opposite each other on a crossroads with no other signs of civilization in sight. Apparently there was a long-standing feud between the two families who owned them, and if you were seen going in one you were barred entry to the other.

We rented RVs to sleep in and the Record Plant Truck to record the proceedings. The house made a wonderful studio. All the rooms were lined with wood, which made for great acoustics. Overall I have very fond memories of the whole experience. Another band with a great vocal blend. The music was great, as was the company. Can't ask for much more, really. Except maybe edible food.

The album was released and we reached number three in America with the first single, "Jackie Blue." The song had not even been submitted by the band as possible material for the record because it supposedly made reference to some drug, but I heard Larry Lee playing it on the piano in a lunch break, and being completely ignorant of the drug connotation I got very excited, dragging everyone back into the room to record it immediately.

I had a disagreement over the content of the second album with Stanley Plesser, the band's manager—a man who should have stuck to selling shoes, in my opinion. This resulted in me quitting and leaving the band in David's very capable hands for their third album.

Eventually David relinquished his desire to be a member of staff without portfolio and in 1984 took on the job of supervising movie music for the company for a few years. Among his many successes were *Pretty in Pink, The Breakfast Club,* and the hugely successful *Good Morning, Vietnam.* Then, in 1989, he succumbed to pressure from Jerry and finally took the job of head of A&R at A&M, where he ran the department with great success for ten years until the company was finally sold in 1999 to Vivendi, to become part of the Universal group.

Mimi, Jan, and Bob, July 1969

I n June, having delivered Steve's Beatle boots, we went in to record *Your Saving Grace*. On the evening of July 3rd, I was working in the studio with the Steve Miller Band when there was a polite knock on the control room door, which I opened to reveal a stunningly beautiful young woman. She apologized for the intrusion and, having introduced herself as Mimi Fariña, explained that she had just heard that Brian Jones had died that day. Having been told that I was in town working with Steve, she felt obliged to come and break the sad news to me in person.

I was shocked and saddened at the news, which was somewhat mitigated by Mimi's being so kind and thoughtful as to take the time to come and deliver it. I soon learned that she was a wonderful folksinger, having made two albums with her husband, Richard Fariña, in the mid-sixties. The partnership was brought to a sudden end when he was tragically killed in a motorcycle accident in 1966. As a solo artist, she found herself in the shadow of her sister Joan Baez, the American queen of folk. However, later that year she joined forces with Tom Jans and made an album for A&M.

In later life Mimi established and ran Bread & Roses, a charitable organization that provides free entertainment for the institutionalized, initially in San Francisco and now all over America. She spent her entire adult life selflessly giving to others, until she died from cancer in 2001.

During the last few days working with Steve I was invited to stay with Jann Wenner, the founder of *Rolling Stone* magazine. We had been introduced by Steve Miller and Boz Scaggs on my first visit to San Francisco.

Phil Walden had arranged for me to go to Georgia to meet with the Allman Brothers when I had finished with Steve Miller, to discuss the possibility of me producing their first album. I told Jann where I was going and he decided to accompany me, as apparently our mutual friend Boz was there and Jann had become concerned about his well-being for some reason.

I went to see the Allman Brothers in rehearsal and felt that they were not ready to make an album yet. It was very early days for them. They clearly had potential, but were still a little rough round the edges. For some reason they had decided to use two drummers in the band. This is not an easy thing to pull off, and they were still figuring out how to play with each other. This made the rhythm section quite stiff and unsettled, which was the reason I passed. Duane Allman took me back to his house for the evening, and we hit it off instantly and had a great time talking about music and musicians until the early hours. He was a lovely man, as well as a phenomenal guitar player.

Jann and I flew on to New York. During the flight, he was editing an interview he had recently done with Bob Dylan. It was something of a coup, as Dylan had not been interviewed for several years.

We landed in New York, and while walking through the baggage claim area we spotted none other than Dylan himself, leaning against a pillar, people-watching. Jann went over to talk to him while I collected my luggage and went outside to find the limousine that was meeting us. I had never met Dylan, and left them alone to talk. The next thing I knew, Jann was tapping me on the shoulder and there was the great man himself, having come over to say hi. He asked me about the Beatles album I had just finished and was very complimentary about my work with the Stones over the years. In turn, I babbled on about how much we had all been influenced by his work. He said he had this idea to make a record with The Beatles and the Stones, and asked me if I would find out whether the others would be interested.

I was completely bowled over. Can you imagine, the three greatest influences on popular music in the previous decade making an album together?

As soon as I got back to England, I rang everyone to see if they would agree to such an idea. Keith and George both thought it was fantastic, but then they would since they were both huge Dylan fans. Ringo, Charlie, and Bill were amicable to the idea as long as everyone else was interested. John didn't say a flat no, but he wasn't that interested. Paul and Mick both said absolutely not.

I have often wondered whether it would have worked. It certainly would not have been easy. I had it all figured out. We would pool the material from Mick & Keith, Paul & John, Bob, and George, and then select the best rhythm section from the two bands to suit whichever song we were cutting. Paul and Mick were probably right, however I would have given anything to have given it a go. Many years later, Dylan had his wish partially granted when he and George Harrison put the Traveling Wilburys together with Roy Orbison, Jeff Lynne, and Tom Petty.

Six weeks after the chance meeting at LaGuardia Airport, I finally got to work with Dylan when his first producer, Bob Johnston, asked me to record him live at the Isle of Wight Festival. He was being backed by The Band. Their first album, *Music from Big Pink*, had become a massive influence on my musical taste, so this was to be a treat indeed.

The night before the gig, I was invited to go to a rehearsal in the ballroom of the enormous house they had rented on the island. This was an evening I will never forget. I sat alone in the middle of this large ornate ballroom on one of the gilded wooden chairs that littered the room, and was privy to a performance of a substantial part of the set they were to play the following day, and to their process of refining it to what I thought was perfection to start with. The concert itself was not as great. After less than an hour, Mr. Dylan got the hump and decided to leave. I think a couple of tracks were eventually used but I never heard them.

M y next meeting with Bob Dylan was in 1984, when Bill Graham, who was managing him at the time, invited me to produce a live album *Real Live*, while he was on tour in Europe. Mick Taylor and Ian McLagan were in the band and I had not seen either of them for some years. I was a little wary of seeing Mick after my last experience of him with the Stones, but I was pleasantly surprised when I met him again. He seemed to be a reformed character.

Some of the members of Dylan's crew were unbelievably rude and uncooperative when I arrived in France to record the first gig. I was virtually thrown off the stage when I went to place my mics, and it was only the intervention of Bill Graham that prevented me from leaving there and then. The level of security around Dylan was ridiculous. I never quite discovered if it was because he employed a bunch of self-important arseholes, or if it was just his policy in order to preserve his privacy. I had never been in a situation that did not allow me to have a discussion with the artist I was working with before starting the project.

Halfway through his set he would take a breather, leave the stage, and let the band do a song. Having not been allowed anywhere near him since I arrived, I decided that I would leave my truck at this point and catch him in the wings for a chat. Surprisingly, he was really charming and quite happy to discuss what we were doing, albeit briefly, before returning to the stage to complete the set. From then on, access was easier and I was able to keep him up to date with how we were doing from one performance to the next.

We recorded five or six concerts all over Europe, ending up at Slane Castle in Ireland. The night before the gig, the local police station had been blown up by the IRA, so that was a little disconcerting, but I remember it was a fine summer's day with the only negative being that a fan had drowned in the river bordering the property while trying to gain free access to the concert. Bono came and visited me in the truck to say hi before joining Dylan on stage to sing "Blowin' in the Wind," which I might add he did not know the lyrics to. This did not discourage him in any way from making unintelligible sounds throughout. No one seemed to notice, as the performance received rapturous applause from the adoring fans. Perhaps my inability to remember lyrics would not have been a problem after all.

Dylan returned to America when we finished, and I went home to do rough mixes of all the concerts to send to him so that we could discuss which songs and performances we should use on the record. Though we agreed on the songs, it turned out that he had a completely different idea about the performances, with him picking easily the worst examples of each track. I will never know if this was a test of some sort, but in my opinion the versions he chose were unusable. We spent several evenings on the phone talking about all manner of things. He was extremely pleasant and respectful, as in the end he agreed to use the takes that I was suggesting.

Having finished the mixes in my studio at home, I took them to L.A. to master with Doug Sax at the Mastering Lab. This is the process for transferring the music from tape to disc.

Out of courtesy, I asked Bob if he would like to attend, as he lived in L.A. It turned out that he had never been to a mastering session before and happily came along to check the process out. He stayed till the end of the session, then shook my hand and thanked me as I walked him out to his car. This turned out to be the most beaten-up, old convertible Cadillac I have ever seen, with virtually no paint left on the rusting body. So with a smile and a wave, he drove off into the afternoon sun, heading west down Hollywood Boulevard, and sadly, I have never seen him since.

Sixties Sum-Up, Howlin' Wolf, Humble Pie, *Mad Dogs*, *Sticky Fingers*, "Gimme Shelter," and "Sympathy for the Devil"

The sixties started with almost everything being recorded in mono on quarter-inch tape, in three-hour sessions. Singles were what sold. An album, if you were lucky enough to make one, would be done in a day in three separate three-hour sessions, rarely finishing after 10:30 p.m., and never during weekends. Artists hardly ever wrote their own material, so therefore songwriters were just that and hardly ever performed their own songs. The industry was run by a small number of corporate labels, who employed staff A&R men to sign and produce the talent.

By the time the sixties were over, we were up to sixteen tracks on two-inch tape and albums were responsible for 80 percent of record sales, sometimes taking months to make, with everyone working seven days a week and very often all night. A&R men were confined to signing the talent and retaining an independent producer to make the record. The money advanced on signing a record contract had gone through the roof, with the deal almost certainly negotiated by a new breed of lawyer that had not existed ten years previously. The single was fast becoming just a promotional tool to sell albums, and the album sleeve had become an art form. All this driven by a massive increase of profits in the industry perhaps by as much as tenfold.

1970 started with a party at Ringo's house on New Year's Day. My overriding memory of that evening is hearing the sound of drums being played in another room in the house. I went to investigate and found Keith Moon giving Ringo's four-year-old son, Zak, a lesson. Zak idolized Keith, who was his godfather. Amazingly, twenty-five years later he took Keith's place in The Who, being one of the few drummers in the world who could come close to filling his shoes.

The first week of January was spent wrapping up *Let It Be* at Abbey Road and Olympic, and the Billy Preston album with George Harrison. Then I was off to the States for a couple of months, darting between L.A. and San Francisco, working with Steve Miller, Leon Russell, and a co-production with David Anderle for A&M with Lambert and Nuttycombe, a folk duo from Carmel Valley in Northern California. Their music was smooth and very laid-back, delivered with a wonderful blend of two-part harmony. They were great at what they did but sadly did not manage to catch the eye or ear of the public.

I returned home at the end of March to start a grueling couple of weeks of all-nighters with The Rolling Stones and the first few sessions with Peter Frampton and Steve Marriott from the Small Faces, for Humble Pie's first album. Not the most innovative album title.

Then I received a call from Chess Records, asking if I would engineer some sessions at Olympic Studios with the blues legend Howlin' Wolf. The great man was going to rerecord his most famous songs with the young English upstarts of the day who had taken the music business in Britain and America by storm, invariably using the black man's blues as a vehicle. I could not pass up the opportunity.

The experience proved to be extraordinary in several ways. First, how the guy from Chess ever got to be a record producer is beyond me. He proved to be totally incompetent on just about every level. He had the personality of a dead fish, and it quickly became obvious to me that he knew absolutely nothing about the blues.

In an attempt to be as commercial as possible, he booked Ringo Starr and Klaus Voormann as the rhythm section. I am a huge fan of both these musicians but neither of them would know anything about the blues if they fell over them. I have no idea why they even agreed to do the sessions, particularly as Ringo came to me on the first day and asked me what the hell he was doing there, asking if I could help to get him and Klaus out of their commitment to the rest of the sessions. I suggested to the producer that he had made a mistake in booking them and perhaps I could persuade Bill Wyman and Charlie Watts to come with Stu and play on the rest of the sessions. That night I rang Bill at his home in Suffolk, a couple of hours outside London. He was not that interested in coming to town the next day until I told him who the artist was. Like Stu and Charlie, he dropped everything and jumped in the car, thrilled at the opportunity to meet and play with the great man. Thank God they were available. So Ringo and Klaus were excused.

The producer had contributed virtually nothing to the first session, and I felt, if anything, he was an obstruction to the proceedings. The next night with Charlie, Stu, and Bill present, things took a turn for the better, until he decided to play the band the original version of the song we were about to cut. He went to the turntable in the control room and put the record on and sat down and listened without realizing that it was playing at the wrong speed. That was the last straw for me and I banned him from the control room, asking him to stay in the studio with the musicians or wait in the hall.

Wolf was a big man with a chest the size of a barrel and huge hands with fingers that appeared to be far too fat to play the guitar. His speaking voice was deep and sounded like someone had poured a couple of pounds of ground glass down his throat. He would sit in the control room with me while the musicians were learning the song in the studio and would tell me stories, explaining the lyrics he had written. I am embarrassed to admit that I did not understand a great deal of what he said, as he had an almost unintelligible accent. I would sit fascinated and enthralled, never letting on, trying desperately to interpret what he was telling me but not wishing to appear rude by asking him to repeat what he was saying. He was a gentle giant and I felt so privileged to be in his presence.

The saddest thing about the whole experience was Wolf seemingly had no idea why he was there. He may have known who Eric Clapton was, but that was only because someone had told him. He did not seem to know who any of the other musicians were. It looked to me like he was being manipulated for commercial purposes by his label, without having much of a clue about what was going on. He was elderly, confused, and not in the best of health.

The finest moment of the sessions came when we were about to cut "Little Red Rooster." This song and the guitar riff it is based on were trademarks of Wolf's and had been covered by the Stones quite early on.

The musicians started to run it down when Wolf stopped them, came into the control room, opened his beat-up cardboard guitar case, and took out an ancient, equally beat-up F-hole acoustic guitar.

He took the guitar into the studio and sat down opposite Eric, looking him fair and square in the eye, and said, "I am going to teach you how to play this. Somebody has to do it right after I am gone."

I ran to the tape machine and hit record as soon as I realized what was happening and recorded the old master teaching the young, awestruck pretender. It was an epic moment for all in the room.

Eric was hugely respectful to Howlin' Wolf and a big fan of Hubert Sumlin, the guitar player on most of the original tracks. He frequently said to the producer that he did not understand why the record was being made, as the definitive versions of all the songs already existed and he felt under enormous pressure to compete with them in some way. Particularly as Hubert Sumlin was present in the control room with me on some of the sessions.

When we had finished recording I declined the request for me to mix the record, as the idea of spending any time in a room alone with the producer was quite abhorrent. I am sure he felt the same about me. So he took the tapes back to America and added some overdubs and mixed it there. I do not own a copy and have never listened to it, so I don't know if he managed to ruin it, but I would suggest it is well worth checking out.

. . .

The next day I started an album with Jesse Ed Davis, the phenomenal Native American guitar player from Taj Mahal's band. We met and got on really well while working on the Stones' *Rock and Roll Circus*, so when he returned to England in May, I was happy to help him with a few sessions at Olympic for his first solo album.

This was followed by finishing the Humble Pie album, mixing *Stage Fright* for The Band, and a further month of all-nighters with the Stones and Jimmy Miller, working on *Sticky Fingers*, with a two-week trip to L.A. in the middle for good measure, to work at A&M studios for Jerry Moss on Joe Cocker's *Mad Dogs & Englishmen*.

The Rolling Stones had commissioned a state-of-the-art mobile recording unit in a truck and had given the job to Stu to organize. He in turn came to me for advice and assistance. In late September, the truck was finally finished and ready to test. So we took it to Paris to record the Stones in concert. Unfortunately the trip was wasted, as neither of the two 16-track tape machines that Stu had got some kind of deal on proved to be operable.

A week after we returned from Paris, I was sent to New York to mix the music for the Maysles brothers' documentary *Gimme Shelter*. They had shot the Stones' American tour late in '69 and I was to mix the music for all the footage of them playing. I had been on most of the tour and had recorded the live album *Get Yer Ya-Ya's Out!* at what was supposed to be the last two gigs in Baltimore and finally at Madison Square Garden in New York. The Stones had come up with the idea of doing a free concert in San Francisco and had hurriedly tacked it on the end of the tour. So the day after Madison Square Garden, they all flew back to the West Coast to play at Altamont

Speedway and I went home to England to attend my son Ethan's christening the next day.

So, eleven months later I found myself being ushered into a darkened office in New York by Albert and David Maysles in order for them to show me the finished edit of their film. One of them turned the projector on as they left the room, saying they would wait for me in the outer office.

I thought I was going to see a movie about the tour: the usual backstage stuff in the dressing room before the show, the band getting on and off planes and into limos, with the odd footage of them playing in concert. However, I was taken completely by surprise as they had really made a film about the horrific events that took place at Altamont. I had been told in some detail about what happened that day by Stu and the band and felt extremely fortunate that I had missed the whole experience. Someone had the bright idea to get the local chapter of the Hells Angels to provide security around the extremely low, unprotected stage and pay them in beer. It did not take long for the violence that they are associated with to take over as they set about the crowd with pool cues and eventually stabbed a man to death right in front of the stage. Seeing what actually happened on the screen was far more disturbing than any oral account I had heard.

I was one of the first people to see the film, and the brothers were waiting in the outer office with great anticipation to see my reaction to it. Which was not at all as they had expected. I came into the room having been seriously upset by what I had just seen, and stated that they could not possibly release it the way it was, as kids would go and see it assuming, as I had, that they were to see a movie about their favorite band and their music. My reaction was completely over-the-top; when the film was eventually released it was not promoted in a misleading way. I don't blame the Maysles brothers at all for what they did. They decided to tag along to Altamont and what happened there ended up being far more thought provoking than anything they had shot on the road in the previous weeks. Their movie showed the arrogance and total incompetence of those who put together the free show at Altamont Speedway, resulting in some extreme violence, a murder, and an ugly end to the drug-induced "peace and love" movement of the late sixties. Which, in retrospect, may not be a bad thing.

The song being played when the violence in the crowd kicked off was "Sympathy for the Devil." Mick went across the stage to Keith and asked him to stop playing so that he could try and calm the audience down, announcing as they started playing again, "Something very funny always happens when we start playing that number."

In fact, there had been another scary incident that took place while this song was being played. In the early summer of 1968, the French director Jean-Luc Godard convinced the band to be filmed for his movie *One Plus One* while the Stones were recording "Sympathy for the Devil" at Olympic Studios. Godard seemed a very strange little man to me and spent two nights shooting the same tracked camera run over and over again while the band worked on the song. In the middle of a take on the second night, the session was brought to an abrupt halt by a huge neon light fitting falling from the ceiling, missing Keith Richards by inches. It would most certainly have killed him if he had been standing a couple of feet to his right.

Having been built as a cinema, the Olympic had an extremely high ceiling and the film crew had managed to set some very powerful lights alongside the massive neon light fittings that already existed there. They had then placed a large plastic sheet over the lot in order to diffuse the light. This had created an enormous build-up of heat that had eventually caused the ceiling and the roof above it to catch fire.

Once we realized what was happening, a mild panic took over, with everyone running round like ants figuring out how best to deal with an attack on the nest. If you haven't noted the whereabouts of the fire extinguishers near you in your place of work, I strongly recommend that you do, as you will most certainly deal with any incident involving a fire far more calmly and efficiently than I did.

I grabbed the extinguisher off the wall in the control room, and when I finally figured out how to work it, the jet didn't even reach halfway to the raging inferno in the ceiling and all I achieved was a wet puddle on the floor. It transpired that compressed straw had been used as sound insulation in the roof of the building, which needed to be particularly effective as it was directly under the flight path to Heathrow. We quickly managed to get all of the Stones' gear out of the building while the film crew did the same with theirs. All this action being filmed with a handheld 16-millimeter camera by Godard, who stood calmly in the doorway with a disconcerting smile on his face.

The fire department arrived and dealt with the problem by bravely sending firemen up into the roof space from inside the building, while we all stood in the street, watching the flames leap into the night sky.

Incredibly, the studio was operational by the following afternoon when Keith Grant had an orchestral session. We followed him in at 7:30 in the evening, and other than the smell of fire and the blackened hole in the ceiling, the previous night's drama was soon forgotten. It still gives me the creeps whenever I hear that song.

The rest of the year was taken up with finishing the Humble Pie album, recording the first McGuinness Flint album, and making the first of two albums with Boz Scaggs in San Francisco. He was signed to CBS, and in those days they had the ridiculous union policy of only allowing their engineers to record the product for their label, having only just agreed to let their artists record in a studio of their choice rather than one that belonged to the company. As I always engineered what I produced, this was a bit of a problem that was only overcome by the generosity of the guy they sent to San Francisco to do the sessions, who happily agreed to sit at the back of the room for the duration. This restrictive practice, plus the fact that they paid considerably less in royalties than anyone else in the business, kept me well away from them after I had finished with Boz.

This eventually resulted in me being invited to New York by Clive Davis in order for him to convince me that I was making a huge mistake by refusing to work for CBS. He was running the company and was well on the way to his "guru" status in the industry and more especially in his own eyes. I have never met anyone with quite such a high opinion of himself. He told me that even though CBS paid a third less than anyone else in the industry at that time I would make more money with them, as they sold more records than anyone else. Summoning teams of sycophantic administrators to unravel piles of royalty statements from Janis Joplin's latest release on the desk in front of me in his palatial office to prove the point. I could not wait to leave, returning to my hotel feeling like I needed a long hot shower. All he managed to do was confirm that my original decision was correct.

By now, many studios were beginning to modernize. Most of the great rooms had been built in the fifties and early sixties, and as methods of recording changed with the advent of more and more tracks becoming available to record on, the consoles were becoming outdated and the transistor was taking over from valves, changing the sound. The transistor was much smaller, so the new equipment could be made more compact, and as a result much more could be crammed in, and it was far more reliable, not generating the heat that tubes do. As with most modernization, there was a price to pay. The musicality and warmth of recorded sound suffered, and the equipment became more and more complex. Unnecessarily so, in my view.

I was asked by Jerry Wexler at Atlantic Records to have a meeting with him in New York regarding the redesign of their studio. Jerry was a legend in the music business and had played a major role in the success of Atlantic Records as a staff producer, working closely with the founders of the label, Ahmet and Nesuhi Ertegun. He is credited with inventing the phrase "rhythm and blues" when working as a journalist at *Billboard* magazine before starting with Atlantic in 1953 at the age of forty-six.

I had never used the studio but it had a fantastic reputation. Countless wonderful records had been made there with artists like Aretha Franklin, Ray Charles, John Coltrane, and Charlie Mingus, to name just a few. Great jazz and R&B records, representing an entire era of popular American music, had been absorbed by the walls of those rooms.

The genius engineer and producer Tom Dowd had been on the staff for years. As a result, they were always ahead of everyone else technically, being the first studio to record in stereo and the first to use multitrack recording. So I arrived for the meeting with some trepidation, having never met Jerry and feeling like I was stepping on hallowed ground as I entered the building. Jerry Wexler proved to be charming and soon put me at ease, showing me round the studio while explaining that they had come to the decision that it should be updated to keep up with the latest trends in recording. I respectfully made a few suggestions about equipment and control room layout but told him that in my opinion it would be sacrilege to touch the rooms, as I was already finding it more and more difficult to find facilities that were suited to the kind of live recording that I did. I was incredibly flattered to have been sought out by Jerry and Tom Dowd for my input, as minimal as it turned out to be.

I can only assume that the reason they had contacted me was because of my work with the Stones and the fact that I had just made the first Led Zeppelin album, which Atlantic had recently acquired for release. If that was the case, what they seemed not to grasp was that this supposedly new rock and roll sound came from the musicians, not from any new innovative recording process.

Studios that were built in the next twenty years invariably incorporated design that led to the complete isolation of musicians and their instruments, one from another. This, along with the ability to overdub on an ever-increasing number of tracks, was the seed that eventually became the common practice of layering—recording one instrument at a time. In the old days, existing buildings were converted, and acoustics of the rooms were adjusted by trial and error by the engineers that were using them. The new breed of designers used engineers to supposedly create the perfect acoustic environment, resulting invariably with rooms with no character or individuality and that had very little to do with musicality. Having started when everything had to be recorded at once, I have never lost the value of musicians interacting with one another as they play. This can be so subtle, and invariably is nothing more than a subconscious emotive reaction to what others are playing around you, with what you are contributing having the same effect on them. When a musician overdubs his or her part onto an existing track, this ceases to be a two-way reaction. With only the musician who is added being affected by what he or she is playing to. Recording equipment was originally designed to capture the performance of a piece of music. Now it influences the way music is written and performed.

No process should stand still, and I take my hat off to those who have contributed to the modern methods of recording. Undoubtedly, the creative process has benefited enormously in many ways. My only plea is that the methods I was taught are not ignored and forgotten, as this would be a great loss to the recorded performance of contemporary music of any era.

The Who and Neil
Young, 1971

No one should ever underestimate the influence that Pete Townshend has had on popular music. There is no question in my mind that both he and The Who were every bit as influential as The Beatles and the Stones as the UK invasion took America and the rest of the world by storm. He was equally as innovative as a musician and lyricist, finding a way to state the feelings of the mod generation he and the band represented. The combination of these four unlikely cohorts interpreting Pete's writing was something to behold, each of them contributing in his own original way. The seemingly uncontrolled explosion of energy they produced, glued together by exceptional musicianship.

In January '71, I returned from L.A. to find that Pete Townshend had written to me, asking if I would be interested in helping him with his next project, a film and a soundtrack album he had written called *Lifehouse*. He enclosed a script and the demos of the songs he had written.

I had waited years for this invitation. I had known the band from the beginning when they were called The High Numbers. They were on the same circuit as The Presidents, and on odd occasion we were on the same bill. This resulted in us forming a mutual appreciation society and me forming a friendly connection with Pete. So you can imagine my surprise and pleasure when a couple of years later they turned up along with Shel Talmy at IBC as The Who with a revolutionary new sound and me as the engineer. I was lucky enough to record a few of the early singles they did with Shel, including "My Generation."

When Kit Lambert and Chris Stamp took over their management, they took issue with Shel's contract to produce them, with it eventually ending up in court, where I appeared as a witness for Shel. This was a difficult decision to make, as I was asked to appear for both sides of the dispute. In those days it was quite normal for a producer to have a contract that lasted several years, the principle being that he would have helped establish the act with his expertise and therefore was entitled to a royalty for the term of the contract, whether he continued working with them or not. I took Shel's side based on the fact that they were breaking an agreement without any fault on Shel's part, as far as I could see. As a result, The Who and I went our separate ways, until a few years later when I ran into them at an NME Awards show at Wembley Arena in London. Roger Daltrey came over to say hi and explained that as a result of me taking Shel's side in the lawsuit they had lost, since a major part of their case for breaking the contract was based on the fact that I was producing the sessions and therefore Shel was not. I had no idea that was the case, but I still feel I made the right decision, although it did return to bite me in the arse, as when it came time for me to negotiate my deal as their producer a few years later, I was given a much reduced royalty, because as Shel had won the case, he still had a piece of the action. At least that was the reason I was given by an extremely pissed-off Kit Lambert, who I was replacing in the job. It transpired that there had already been an aborted attempt at recording the album in New York, with Kit producing.

So having finally been approached by Pete to produce the band, I willingly agreed to his suggestion to meet up at his house with him, Roger Daltrey, Keith Moon, John Entwistle, and Bill Curbishley, who was representing the management, to discuss how to proceed with the project. We started to talk about the film, and feeling totally inadequate, I owned up to the fact that I did not understand the story in the script. Embarrassingly, one by one, everyone else in the room said the same. This was pointed out with much respect to Pete, and I certainly saw it as my failure and not a criticism of what he had written. There seemed to be little appetite for the film from the band and it was agreed that the movie should be dropped and that we go ahead with the album, as the material would stand up on its own with or without the movie.

The demos that Pete had sent us were amazing. Unlike so many demos, these left very little to the imagination. Great songs. Beautifully recorded with complex arrangements, and instrumentation featuring the innovative use of synthesizers. The very fact that he figured out how to get one to work in those early days, never mind use it as effectively as he did, has always amazed me. He had a studio at home and had become an extremely accomplished engineer. Throughout my involvement with the band I was permanently in-

timidated by Pete's demos, as I was constantly challenged to make
what we did sound as good or better than the original. Very often I
would steal elements from his original recording and use them as a
track for the band to play to.

The day after the meeting at Pete's house I went to L.A. to master
the Humble Pie album I had just finished, wrap up my work on the
Joe Cocker *Mad Dogs & Englishmen* movie, and mix something for
the Stones at Sunset Sound before returning home to start mixing *Songs for Beginners* for Graham Nash. Having released their
number-one album *Déjà Vu* the previous year, featuring that extraordinary blend of four completely different voices, Crosby, Stills,
Nash & Young all went their separate ways and made equally successful solo albums, writing and performing their own songs. Their
contribution to the evolution of popular music being all the more
extraordinary with each of them having been in groundbreaking
bands before they got together. Stephen and Neil coming from Buf-
falo Springfield, Graham Nash from The Hollies, and David Crosby
from The Byrds.

I enjoyed working with Graham, being really impressed by his
solo efforts and getting to know him much better over the three days
it took to mix his album, and it was by complete coincidence that
I went to Barking Town Hall in London the next day to record "A
Man Needs a Maid" and "There's a World" with Neil Young and the
London Symphony Orchestra for what became the *Harvest* album.
We used the Stones' mobile recording unit, or the Stones Truck as it
became known. This is one of the few occasions I got to record a symphony orchestra, having witnessed it on many occasions when I was
training. I am not quite sure what the orchestra made of the disheveled, somewhat unkempt character that sat down at the piano at ten
a.m. that morning, although on a visit to the men's room during the

first union break, I did overhear some disparaging remarks from two members of the orchestra while standing at the urinal.

Jack Nitzsche, the American producer, arranger, musician, and songwriter, had done the arrangements, and during the first run-through of "A Man Needs a Maid," it became apparent that conducting a symphony orchestra was not one of his many talents. It was a mess. Jack's method was entirely out of sync with these classical guys, and as the last chord died away, the room was filled with an ominous, somewhat disgruntled murmuring from the orchestra. A male violinist in the second fiddles put his hand up and asked Jack politely if he could approach. I jumped out of the truck and ran into the hall, getting to the conductor's podium just as the man arrived, thinking I could arbitrate should that become necessary. The man was charming and politely whispered to Jack that it was apparent that he did not have any experience conducting a symphony orchestra, and offered to take over, as he was a conductor. Jack readily agreed, and with much relief stepped down, giving his baton to the violinist. From then on, the session went like a dream, the results being there for all to hear. It was a fabulous experience, made all the better by it being with Neil and the two wonderful songs he wrote.

The Stones at the
Marquee Club

The rest of March 1971 was taken up with starting and completing the second album with McGuinness Flint and recording the Stones live in concert at a couple of venues around the UK and for a TV show that never saw the light of day. The Stones played a gig at the famous Marquee Club on Wardour Street in London's Soho for the sole purpose of producing a TV show of them playing live.

The choice of venue was perfect, as it was a small club, famous for promoting the start of the blues movement in England. Nearly everyone who was anyone had played there at the beginning of their career, including the Stones on several occasions. They had done a deal with a small production company that provided the crew and equipment, and I was required to record the sound, once again using the Stones' mobile truck.

We arrived at midday to set up, ready for a three p.m. start. The place was packed with an audience brimming with anticipation at seeing their favorite band up close for the first time in years. At three p.m. everyone was there and ready to go except Keith Richards. No surprise there. He eventually arrived, having to barge his way through the audience to get to the stage, as the only way in was through the front of the building. So after a long wait we were ready to go. The band was a few minutes into the set when an irate Harold Pendleton, the owner of the club, came pushing through the crowd, screaming something about how his Marquee Club signs had been moved and were not in shot. This supposedly had been part of the agreement with him allowing the place to be used for the show. Not many people I ever met liked Harold very much, and Keith saw his opportunity to settle old scores and threatened to flatten him with his guitar if he did not leave. So Harold retreated back into the crowd, not to be seen again that day.

The next interruption came with a loud banging on the door of my truck, which when opened revealed a large policeman demanding to know whose car it was that had been left in the middle of the street with the engine running. It turned out to belong to Keith. Having arrived as late as he did and not finding a parking place, he just got out of the car, leaving it where it was in the middle of the street, and went into the club. By the time he had fought his way to the stage, he had completely forgotten to tell anyone to go and park it for him. It must have been there for at least twenty minutes and was causing chaos to the traffic in Soho.

From there on, things seemed to be going okay until they got about forty minutes into the set, when they were to play "Wild Horses." Keith took his twelve-string guitar and sat down with his legs dangling over the front of the stage and began to check its tuning. For the next few minutes we were treated to the sound of him struggling to get it in tune, while everyone stood patiently around, until suddenly it went quiet. I looked up at my monitor in the truck to see Keith sitting with the guitar in his hands and his head dropped down on his chest, asleep.

Mick immediately announced that it was all over. The performance was finished. The disappointed audience was ushered out. I went in with my crew and packed up our gear. After around an hour or so, with the TV crew in the final throes of striking their equipment, Mick, Charlie, and I were standing on the stage with our coats on, discussing what we would do the following day, when all of a sudden we heard the sound of a twelve-string guitar being tuned. Keith, who had not moved and had been completely ignored by everyone since falling asleep, had woken up and continued tuning as if nothing had happened, completely oblivious to the fact that the houselights were on and the place was empty, all but for the few remaining members of the TV crew packing up.

Who's Next

T he previous year, 1970, the Stones had started recording at Mick Jagger's house out in the country, near Newbury. By this time, the Stones Truck was fully operational and we used the huge entrance hall of the Victorian pile that was Stargroves to record several tracks that were eventually used on *Sticky Fingers*. I had mentioned to Pete Townshend in conversation that these sessions had gone really well, so he suggested that we go there to start recording *Who's Next*.

We began on the first day with "Won't Get Fooled Again." Not a bad way to start. With Pete's permission, I edited the synthesizer track from his original demo, as it was a little too long, and played it in to the band in the studio. They performed live to it with remarkable skill, the synthesizer dictating a constant tempo for every bar of the song, with them staying locked relentlessly to it throughout. Roger Daltrey's powerful vocal equaled the energy of the band, capping the whole thing off with that amazing scream just before the end of the song.

I have a residing memory of sitting in the truck, my hair being parted by what was coming out of the speakers, a massive amount of adrenaline coursing through my veins. There have been a few occasions over the years when I have been completely blown away, believing without a doubt that what I was listening to would become much more than just commercially successful but also a marker in the evolution of popular music, and this was one of those moments.

The novelty of recording at Stargroves only lasted two days and was soon replaced by the convenience of Olympic, where we worked for the next two weeks, it only being a short drive away for everyone each day. Some of the songs required a slightly more conventional approach than John and Keith were used to, so tailoring them to suit the band without losing the essence of the way they had been written became a bit of a problem. We achieved this in various ways. Making Keith's kit smaller and getting John to play with more weight to his sound being two of them. I felt a bit like I was treading on hallowed ground. Although both of them would have preferred to have been left alone, they generously tried what I suggested and seemed happy to go along with the end result.

Having worked for thirteen days straight, we decided to take a break and reconvene in a month. So, still not having had a day off since New Year's Eve, fifteen weeks earlier, I went back to L.A., bought a car, and persuaded my pal Ethan Russell to accompany me on a drive across America. What an adventure that was. We arrived in New York ten days later, and Ethan dropped me off at JFK in order for me to fly home in time for me to see my family, and for he and I to meet up with the other guests at Gatwick Airport to fly down to the South of France for Mick Jagger's wedding to Bianca. Mick had very generously rented a plane to take us all to Nice, and a couple of buses to take us on to the reception in Saint-Tropez. The trip there and back being the best part. Most of us knew one another and those who did not soon put that right, everyone determined to have a good time. It was a pretty odd collection of people from all walks of life, like any typical wedding except for a couple of Beatles and the odd member of the Faces thrown in. Everyone was quite raucous on the way there and mostly asleep on the way back, having been up all night.

On my return, I did a couple of days mixing with the Stones and announced that that was it, recommending my brother Andy to take over from me as their engineer. He was eight years younger than me and left school with a burning desire to follow in my footsteps. I managed to get him a job at Olympic, which did not last long, as his timekeeping proved to be less than reliable. However, he moved on and quickly established himself as a formidable engineer, making wonderful-sounding records with, among others, Led Zeppelin, Blind Faith, Jack Bruce, Free, Ten Years After, Jethro Tull, and Cat Stevens. So he was more than qualified to work with the Stones. We never worked together, but I was a huge fan of his sound. I believe that he eventually became the best in the world at recording the heavier side of rock and roll, with Zeppelin's *II, III, IV,* and *Houses of the Holy*, Van Halen, and Joe Satriani.

I started back in with The Who to finish *Who's Next*, finding that you had to be on your toes working with them as they had quite volatile tendencies, but that just made life more interesting. I recall sitting in the control room, discussing what the album should be called, having just finished the first playback of the final running order. Keith Moon's suggestion was *All Their Records*. When asked to explain, he said, "Well, the kids will go into a record store and ask for all their records by The Who."

When it came to the cover, I recommended Ethan Russell, who did the most brilliant job. After a couple of days driving round the south of England with the band, he chanced on the concrete monolith sticking out of a slag heap that became the centerpiece of the now famous cover. The band are walking away, having supposedly urinated on it. Pete Townshend has since claimed that inadvertently it could be viewed as a rebuff for Stanley Kubrick's refusal to direct the movie of *Tommy*.

Denny Cordell and Leon Russell

Denny Cordell got his start in the music business working for Chris Blackwell in 1964, when he was twenty-one years old. He left Island Records to go freelance, having had success producing The Moody Blues, and established a working relationship with David Platz, who owned the music publishing company Essex Music. By the time I met him in 1967, he was a well-respected producer.

He was a striking character, very tall, with a blob of tightly curled hair. He spoke with a cultured, somewhat superior tone that belied his slightly unkempt look. He was extremely assertive on a session and left no one in doubt as to who was in charge. I was amazed to find out recently that he was a year younger than me. I never saw him play an instrument or come up with a musical idea or a part for anyone to play. In fact, I often wondered if he could hold a tune or sing at all. What he did have was a great sense of "feel," and certainly knew a hit when he heard one and how to get the best performance out of any artist.

Our first project was at Olympic, and was an album with The Move, a very successful rock and roll band from Birmingham with whom he had several hits in the sixties.

Next, we worked together on a single for Joe Cocker called "Marjorine." Joe had just arrived on the scene from Sheffield. He turned up at Olympic studio B with his sidekick Chris Stainton, a pale skinny little guy with long lank hair. It turned out that Chris was not only one of the finest keyboard players on the planet but was also an engineer. He was the first musician I can remember to tell me how to record his piano practically before we had said hello, and I am very glad he did, as his method worked brilliantly for the song.

Denny went on to produce Procol Harum's "A Whiter Shade of Pale" at Olympic with Keith Grant engineering, and Joe Cocker's single "With a Little Help from My Friends," both hits making it all the easier to establish himself in America.

He returned to London in September 1969 for me to mix the *Joe Cocker* album, bringing Leon Russell with him. Leon had been working on a solo album at his home in Los Angeles and they decided to continue working on it with me at Olympic. We ended up recutting most of it, and although Leon can play almost any instrument, we brought in a host of great musicians to play on the record: Alan Spenner, the bass player from the Grease Band; Klaus Voormann on bass; Charlie and Bill from the Stones; and Ringo and George from The Beatles, to name but a few.

We didn't mix the record until I returned to Los Angeles in January 1970. It is an extraordinary album. It was great fun to do, and although there is a cast of heavy-duty guys playing on it, Leon still comes across as master of all he surveys.

Denny and Leon formed Shelter Records in 1969, and its first album release was *Leon Russell* in 1970. The label went on to have great success, signing Tom Petty and the Heartbreakers, Phoebe Snow, Freddie King, and JJ Cale. I remember Denny calling me and telling me he had just signed a fantastic band who would be perfect for me to produce once he had made their first album. That was the Heartbreakers. Sadly, it was never to be. They are still one of my favorite bands. There is an upside though. I have often thought that I might well have not done nearly such a good job as whoever went on to produce them and therefore would not enjoy listening to their records nearly as much as I do now. The mystique that comes with listening to a record obviously is not there if you have produced it.

In late June 1970, I got a call from Jerry Moss. He explained that he was in something of a predicament. Joe Cocker, who was probably the biggest male solo artist in America at that time, had gone out on a tour of America with an ensemble put together by Leon Russell and Denny Cordell. Jerry, Denny and Leon had come up with a plan to make both a film of the tour and a live album. They had chosen only two venues to record for the album. The first, right at the beginning of the tour, was the Fillmore East in New York, and the second was right at the end, in Los Angeles. Having listened to the recordings of the two shows, Denny and Leon decided that neither performance was good enough to be used. This meant that there would be no live album and the movie that had been several weeks in the making at some considerable expense was a write-off.

Jerry had suggested that as Denny and Leon were not prepared to continue with the project, would they consider bringing in a third person who they could all agree on, who would be fresh to it all, to try and save it. They had agreed on me.

I was in the middle of the second batch of sessions at Olympic with The Rolling Stones for what became *Sticky Fingers*. Fortunately, they were quite happy for me to go to Los Angeles for a couple of weeks, as we were making the record in fits and starts.

I arrived in L.A. and went straight into A&M Studios to check out the multitrack tapes of the two concerts, and it quickly became apparent that the concert recorded in New York was usable. Eddie Kramer had done a brilliant job recording it, and the band and Joe were still flushed with energy and adrenaline from the freshly rehearsed material. It is quite possible there had been better shows that were not recorded, but my opinion was not tainted by wonderful memories of the gigs that were not recorded, and I thought it was great.

The big problem was the enormous choir. This consisted of six really wonderful singers who had been supplemented by anyone else on the tour who was a friend, hanger-on, groupie, or who had nothing else to do. The result was a cacophony of noise that had little to do with the key that any song was being performed in. I am sure they were all having a great time, but it ruined the recording. However, it was simple to fix. I called Rita Coolidge and asked her to contact the other principle singers, and booked them for the following day to come in and overdub on the entire concert.

Jerry Moss was quite rightly concerned that it should be a double album. This gave me very little leeway to leave anything from the concert off the record. There is a medley that lasts for thirteen and a half minutes that had to be included if I was to meet Jerry's request. Halfway through, there is a key change as it goes into "When Something Is Wrong with My Baby," and as the band reaches a climax Joe attempts one of his marvelous elongated, high, raspy notes. Only, on this occasion all he managed was rasp. This one unfortunate error put the whole thirteen and a half minutes in jeopardy. So I got the choir to sing over it and cover it up, which solved the problem and gave Jerry the double album he wanted.

When I finished, I got Denny and Leon down to studio 1 at Sunset Sound where I had mixed it and tentatively played it back to them. Fortunately, they approved of what I had done and reported back to Jerry that they were quite happy to have the record released.

Throughout this whole process, no one had mentioned Joe. So I called him and asked him to come down to the studio for a playback before I delivered the masters to A&M. It transpired that he had become disenchanted with Denny and Leon and the whole project and had lost any enthusiasm for the record. I told him that I was quite prepared to erase the whole thing if he did not approve it, so he begrudgingly came down to the studio and sat silent and straight-faced through the entire playback, only speaking to utter his approval as he got up to leave.

This turned out to be a very strange project for me. I had been caught in the middle of a disagreement between four individuals, all of whom I respected and considered to be friends. The only happy one when I delivered the finished record was Jerry, who had his album and his movie.

It looked to me like Denny and Leon had used the tour to promote Leon, perhaps to the detriment of Joe. Leon had put the band together and done all the arrangements and was very much the bandleader onstage. So it looked more like the Leon Russell show with Joe as the lead singer. In any event, I had a marvelous time piecing it all together and was greatly inspired by Joe's performance and the music. *Mad Dogs & Englishmen* went on to sell really well, so I am sure that ended up pleasing all concerned.

Denny bought Leon out of Shelter Records in 1976. Once he had started the label it progressively took him away from producing records, which was undoubtedly his forte. Something I would remind him of whenever we met. I felt that we had lost a major talent well before he quit the music business in the late eighties to go and live in Ireland and train horses.

In 1990, I was pleased to hear that he had returned, having found The Cranberries in Ireland, taking them to Chris Blackwell's Island Records. You can't keep a good man down.

So he ended up right where he started, working for Chris, but this time as a traveling A&R man/producer, which he did with great success until he died suddenly in February 1995 from lymphoma.

The Eagles,
1971

In November 1971, I was in Los Angeles and was contacted by David Geffen, who had just started Asylum Records. He had signed the Eagles and set about securing me as the producer for their first record. I had never heard of him or his label, but he was very convincing and assured me that he felt the act would go on to be very successful. He did have Elliot Roberts as a partner, who managed Joni Mitchell and Crosby, Stills, Nash & Young, among others, so that gave him some credibility. I agreed to go to Denver, Colorado, accompanied by John Hartmann from Elliot and David's office to see them play. Unfortunately, there was hardly anyone in the audience; it was a bit unfair really. Not a particularly inspiring situation for them. I have often thought how tricky it must be for any act to play knowing that there is some supposed hotshot producer in the audience who, if things go well, is supposedly going to change their lives by association. There were numerous occasions when I was asked to go and see a band by a record company and the very fact that I had flown several thousand miles for the purpose already made it too big a deal before they had even played a note. I usually knew after a few bars if they were right for me or not, and if they weren't I would spend the rest of the time they were playing trying to figure out how to decline in as pleasant a way as possible without giving offense. There would very often be one guy in the band who would take it the wrong way and become abusive. No matter how you put it, it would end up being really embarrassing for me and the other guys in the band. There is nothing worse than sitting in the middle of an empty room and having a band play for you and you alone, as if you are the arbiter of all taste. I would dread it, and I am sure a lot of the acts dreaded it, too.

The Eagles were at least playing a venue with a few paying members of the public along. They were not that impressive. They played a selection of covers. Chuck Berry rock and roll kind of thing. Bernie Leadon, a great country picker, on one side of the stage, and Glenn Frey, an average rock and roll guitar player on the other, with Don Henley and Randy Meisner being pulled in two directions in the middle. The sound was not that great, and I got no impression of the wonderful vocal harmony that they became famous for. All that, combined with a fairly bland, somewhat awkward stage presence convinced me that they were not worth pursuing, and I returned to London.

I had met Bernie before when he was in The Flying Burrito Brothers with Gram Parsons. I had gone with the Stones to see them play at a small club in Topanga Canyon called the Corral. Keith Richards had a blossoming friendship with Gram. It was a bizarre event, as most were that had anything to do with going anywhere with the Stones. We drove out from Beverly Hills to what seemed like the wilds of Topanga, in a couple of limousines, arriving quite late in the evening to find a handful of people there, most of whom seemed stoned out of their minds.

The most memorable thing about the evening was definitely Gram's voice and Bernie's guitar playing. Other than that, I was bored to tears having to watch a small group of girls who were definitely on acid, dancing—or throwing themselves around, more like—right in front of the table I was sitting at, vying for the attention of any one of the Stones.

David Geffen would not let it go, insisting that I had not seen the Eagles in the best circumstances. He pestered me until I agreed to go back to L.A. and see the band in rehearsal, and thank God that he did.

We spent a morning in a rehearsal facility somewhere in the Valley. They played through the set that I had seen already in Aspen, the result being pretty much the same. We decided to take a break for lunch and as we were exiting the building someone said, "Hold on, before we go, let's just play Glyn 'Most of Us Are Sad,'" a ballad that Randy Meisner sang the lead on, with the others singing harmony. Bernie and Glenn grabbed a couple of acoustic guitars and they played the song without bass and drums, with all of us standing in a group near the door of the building, and there it was. The harmony blend from heaven. It knocked me clean off my feet. In effect, the band had four great lead singers all with completely different voices. When they sang together it created the most wonderful sound.

I am pretty sure we did not break for lunch. We spent the rest of the day exploring the material that they had assembled, during which time it became more and more apparent to me that they were a much better combination of musicians than I had given them credit for. The contrast of Bernie's and Glenn's guitars was really refreshing, with Randy and Don providing a solid and versatile rhythm section for it all to sit on.

I was converted and became quite excited at the prospect of making a record with them, and in equal part felt incompetent for not spotting the potential in the band earlier.

I hung out with them for a few days, going through songs for the album, then went to see them play at the Troubadour, and did a couple of sessions with Rita Coolidge and David Anderle at Elektra Studios. These were the demos that got Rita a record deal with A&M. Then I flew back home to England to start the album the next day with the Eagles at Olympic.

By the time the seventies arrived, you would expect any new act to have a large selection of songs they had written to choose from for their first album. The Eagles had a small pool of strong songs and not all written by them, producing three hit singles: "Witchy Woman," lyrics written by Don Henley and music by Bernie Leadon; "Take It Easy," written by Jackson Browne with assistance in one line of the lyric from Glenn Frey; and "Peaceful Easy Feeling," written by Jack Tempchin. This was early days, and the songwriting partnership of Glenn and Don had not been established yet.

I had a great time making the record, feeling that we were onto something pretty special, and for the most part I thought the band did, too. So they returned to the warmer temperatures of California with what I thought was going to be at the very least a Top 10 album.

The day after I finished with the Eagles, I went straight in with Paul McCartney and Wings to cut the *Red Rose Speedway* album, which I quit in a puff of steam after a couple of weeks, and then went straight on to work with Ronnie Lane and Ronnie Wood on the soundtrack to the movie *Mahoney's Estate*, with our friend, the actor and director Alexis Kanner.

SETUP FOR THE *EAGLES* ALBUM AT OLYMPIC.

Then out of the blue there came a hiccup. David Geffen, having lived with the Eagles' record for a while, felt that we were one Henley vocal short. He was quite right. We had tried to cut the Jackson Browne song "Nightingale" two or three times without success, and I ran out of time and gave up on it. It never came close to working, and I felt we had given it a good shot, and ended up being quite satisfied with the record without it.

One night at three a.m., when I'd just got home and collapsed into bed after a Ronnie Lane and Wood session, Geffen called me from L.A., asking me to go into the studio with the band again and make another attempt at cutting "Nightingale." I explained the situation as politely as I knew how and told him, as disappointing as it was, I felt the record was finished and that although I agreed that another song from Henley would be great, it had not worked out, the performance of the song by the band never came close to being good enough after several attempts, so I had little faith in trying again and therefore could not justify the cost or the logistics involved.

The following night he rang me again, waking me up at exactly the same time in the middle of the night, and we had the same conversation all over again as if the previous night had not happened. This was clearly an attempt to wear me down. He knew perfectly well what time it was in England. So I lost it and told him, as far as I was concerned, the matter was closed, you manage them and I'll produce them and kindly stop ringing and waking me up in the middle of the night.

I finished the soundtrack for the movie and the next day started nine days of sessions with The Who, recording material for what became *Quadrophenia*. The night we were due to finish, I took a surprise call in the control room at Olympic from Bernie Leadon. He and I had become good pals and I was really pleased to hear from him. I was soon to realize that this was not a social call, as he apologetically told me that David Geffen had insisted that they go into the studio in Los Angeles with Bill Halverson, a brilliant and popular local engineer, and make another attempt at recording "Nightingale." This apparently had failed, and Bernie had been given the job of ringing me on behalf of the band, to own up and to ask me yet again if I would have another go at recording the song. To say I was furious is something of an understatement. I expressed my shock and disappointment for the lack of loyalty of the band and hung up the phone.

I had six days before my next project started with the Faces in London, and I had planned to go to L.A. the following day to master a live recording for The Who.

I arrived in Los Angeles the following afternoon and drove from the airport directly to Geffen's office on Sunset Boulevard, still fuming from the previous night's conversation with Bernie. I stormed into his office, rudely brushing past the objections of his assistant outside, to find that he was in the middle of a meeting with the Eagles. How convenient was this? I was able to vent my displeasure to all of them in one hit. Once I had calmed down, the band explained that they had been left no alternative by Geffen. I had refused to recut the song, and he had insisted that he would not release the album without it.

Having poured my heart and soul into the production of this record and thinking that I had the confidence and friendship of the band in the process, I was really disappointed to find that they would go behind my back and record with someone else. This was a hard lesson to learn, but a good one. From that moment on I realized that to have too close a relationship with any artist that I was to work with was almost certainly going to lead to some sort of disappointment. Quite understandably, loyalty becomes far more difficult to maintain for an artist if they believe the future of their career is threatened in any way.

Over the next couple of days I met with Geffen and the band, and having heard the band's point of view along with profuse apologies, I relented and went into Wally Heider's studio in Hollywood and recut the song. It really did not turn out any better, and my original decision to leave it off the record was correct in my opinion. Discretion being the better part of valor, not something I am noted for, I accepted the fact that the song had to go on. In order to appease Geffen.

A distinct positive was, you did get to hear the extraordinary voice of Henley singing lead on two tracks, which was David's whole objective.

At the end of the day, it made little or no difference to the success of the album. I was still quite convinced that we had a massive hit on our hands, and as much as I hate to admit it, thanks to the skills of David Geffen, it was not long before we did. He went into action as soon as we started to make the record, and by the time it was released the word on the street was buzzing with anticipation about the Eagles and their album. The negative aspect of having to deal with David's relentless attempts at getting his own way became a massive positive when he was promoting your product.

The one benefit to come out of having to stay on in L.A. to recut the song was my being invited to go back to Topanga Corral with the band, where they were to play a charity gig. The small club was packed to capacity. We were jammed in like sardines in a tin and very uncomfortable, but it all became worth it when Joni Mitchell came to the stage. This was the first time I had seen her play live and the hairs on the back of my neck still rise when I think about it. I have never heard a voice or a delivery quite like it before or since. She was at her prime.

The very few really great managers that I have come across in the business—Bill Curbishley, Deke Arlon, and John Silva being perfect examples—have left me and the artist alone to get on with the creative decisions regarding the making of an album, and that respect has always been reciprocated, as I would not dream of interfering with the business of the manager steering the artist's career. Not that anyone would be in any way interested in my opinion on such matters.

I had been treating David as a manager who was interfering in the creative process and had not taken into account the fact that he was also their record label, where he had every right to express his dissatisfaction with the finished record. This conflict of interest on his part came to a head with the band when they came to make their next record, *Desperado*. As their manager, he was responsible for getting the best deal possible with their record company. As he was their record company, he was negotiating with himself. Guess who won.

The next time I was in L.A., David asked me to dinner at his house with Jac Holzman and Joni Mitchell. I am not sure to this day what the purpose of this was, but you can rest assured that there was one. It certainly was not because he enjoyed my company. It was already quite obvious that this man would do anything to get his own way. Which, as history will tell you, brought him incredible success in pretty much everything he set his mind on achieving. He has proven over and over again that his taste is remarkable in so many genres of the entertainment business. However, his methods in achieving the end result he desired were not often pleasant.

Jac was a hero of mine. He had started Elektra Records in the 1950s, having shown an insatiable interest in music and the recording process, and has been a major influence on both ever since. I had met him before in London with David Anderle and found him to be charming and a most interesting gentleman.

Joni was at the top of my list of artists to produce. She was making wonderful records with Henry Lewey, another genius engineer/producer in L.A., but there was no harm in wishing.

David knew full well my feelings about Joni, and when she left the room, intimated that if I played my cards right he might be able to facilitate my desire to work with her sometime in the future.

To further wet my whistle, on her return he asked if she would play Jac and me a song that she had just written. I had finished an excellent dinner, seated in a large dimly lit room high up in the Hollywood Hills, with views of the city lights stretching away to the horizon, and Joni Mitchell went to the piano and gave us a private performance of her latest ballad. Whatever David had in mind, it was working. As the last chord of the song died, David suggested that Joni and I go and play pool in another room, as there was something that he wanted to discuss with Jac. I snapped back to reality, feeling a little like a child being sent off to play while the grown-ups talked. In any event, Joni and I had a good time playing pool, and after a while the four of us reconvened and the evening ended with the usual pleasantries.

I never worked with Joni. David had no influence over who she made records with, as she has a very clear mind of her own and she had absolutely no desire to work with me. I suspect that the private conversation with Jac was a precursor to David taking over Elektra and combining it with Asylum the following year.

Desperado and *On the Border*, 1973

H enley and Frey had the idea of making a concept album about the Wild West outlaw gang the Doolin-Daltons. Bernie and I came up with a few musical links to try and tie what there was of a story together, but the concept itself soon dissipated and the strength of the songs they had written carried the record. We had a great time making it, with all the members of the band eagerly contributing to what we believed would be a popular album. I openly encouraged Bernie's and Randy's involvement in the process, as I could see signs of small cracks appearing while Don and Glenn forged ahead in their desire to control the destiny of the band, gently treading on the other two as they went. In any event, they were all so pleased after I had finally assembled and played it back as an entity for the first time that they carried me out of the control room on their shoulders in celebration. However, the euphoria didn't last long as sales sadly did not reach expectations. It was the last

Asylum album to be distributed by Atlantic Records. By this time, David Geffen had much bigger fish to fry. He was in the process of amalgamating his Asylum Records label with Elektra, positioning himself to get on the board of Warner Bros., and had just taken on the management of Bob Dylan. So I think he took his eye off the ball with the Eagles and they did not receive anything like the same attention from him or his label as the first record.

Linda Ronstadt covered and had a huge hit with the title song, "Desperado," but for some reason better known to the gods, the Eagles' version remained an album track. It was not all doom and gloom, as we had two pretty good singles in "Tequila Sunrise" and "Outlaw Man," and the album ended up selling a couple of million. Not to be sneezed at, in my opinion.

The band became disillusioned. Having loved the record when we finished it, they partially blamed me for its lack of success and for it not projecting them into the stratosphere as they had expected. Another lesson learned. If a record is successful it is down to the artist. If not, it's down to the producer. That is quite understandable, and I am sure in some cases it is quite true. Still, it's a difficult pill to swallow when you are on the receiving end of it for the first time. Thereafter I have accepted it as a matter of course.

So when we reconvened at Olympic in late September 1973 to start the third album, *On the Border*, there was already some discontent about me as the producer. Glenn Frey was increasingly frustrated by my not allowing drugs or alcohol in the studio, and Randy Meisner told me that he was unhappy with the sound I was getting. When I asked him to explain, he told me that when he heard an Eagles song on a radio station with poor reception and interference with the signal, it did not sound very good. I thought he was joking, but he was deadly serious. That is a difficult one to deal with.

Glenn and Don wanted a harder rock sound, and as they were not what I considered to be a rock band, I tended to hang on to what I thought was their forte, the harmony vocal sound and the country rock approach to what they were doing. They arrived back at Olympic with very little material and as a pretty disparate bunch. The aforementioned cracks had become larger and there were strong signs of discontent with one another appearing in the band that I did my best to patch up by reminding Frey in particular that they were all as important as each other to the success of the group. It became clear that this is not what he wanted to hear.

The one track we cut that was very much in the vein of what I thought they should be doing was "Best of My Love," which gave them their first number-one hit in America, so I was not entirely wrong. After four weeks, we ground to a halt and decided to take a break, I thought to allow time for them to write more songs. In fact, they returned to America with a new manager and the intent of changing their producer.

In retrospect, it was absolutely the right decision. I was standing in the way of what they wanted to achieve, and the most important role a producer has to play is to help and facilitate, not hinder, exactly that. Their choice of Bill Szymczyk to replace me was an excellent one. He is an engineer with a far more modern approach to recording than me and, I suspect, as a producer, has far more patience. There is no way I could have stayed involved with what followed: fairly heavy substance abuse with hundreds of hours in the studio with the band being at each other's throats, disappearing up their own arses. So I was happy to hand over the baton, wishing Bill all the luck in the world. With Henley and Frey now completely in charge and having cemented their presence as a formidable songwriting team, they added Don Felder and eventually Joe Walsh to give the band a little more edge and the rock and roll feel they were looking for. Although I must admit their idea of rock and roll and mine differ substantially.

I am really proud of the records we made together, and with no disrespect to the others and much admiration for what they have achieved, I still prefer the band as the original four-piece, but then I suppose I would. That harmony blend is as good as it gets.

BACK COVER OF *DESPERADO*. WE ALL GOT TO PLAY
COWBOYS FOR A DAY. FROM LEFT, BACK ROW: GARY BURDEN,
LARRY PENNY, RICHARD FERNANDEZ, BOYD ELDER,
TOMMY NIXON, JOHN HARTMANN AND ME. FRONT ROW:
JACKSON BROWNE, BERNIE LEADON, GLENN FREY, RANDY
MEISNER, DON HENLEY, AND J. D. SOUTHER.

Small Faces/The Faces, 1965–73

The Small Faces and I started working together in 1965 when we recorded their first hit single, "Whatcha Gonna Do About It," at IBC. It was produced by Sammy Samwell, who had gained notoriety as the writer of "Move It," the song that launched Cliff Richard's career. It was not long before they were writing their own songs with the most prolific combination being Ronnie Lane and Steve Marriott. They had several hits, including "Tin Soldier," "Lazy Sunday," and "Itchycoo Park," which became famous for the use of the sound of phasing on one section of the song. I have often been given credit for this, but in fact the method used to achieve it was discovered by my assistant at the time, George Chkiantz, who demonstrated it to me as I arrived for the session. I thought it was a fantastic effect and decided to use it on the track we cut that afternoon. This happened to be "Itchycoo Park," a song about taking

LSD, as coincidence would have it, and if you listen you will see why it was so effective.

I engineered most of their records with them producing. They always had a pretty clear idea of what they wanted, and I would like to think that I helped them achieve it. I think we were a really good team, and although Steve Marriott and I clashed on the odd occasion, we all worked really well together, as we seemed to share the same taste in rock and roll.

This was one hell of a band. They had a massive amount of energy that was unleashed on their audiences from the minute they hit the stage until they left it. If they had ever made it to America, they would undoubtedly have been as successful as any of the British bands that took it by storm in the sixties. That was not to be, as they broke up in 1969 before ever going there.

For the previous couple of years, I had been making the French star Johnny Hallyday's records. His manager would call me and ask me who was hot that month in the UK, and the two English guys who ran his band—guitarist Mick Jones (later of Foreigner) and drummer Tommy Brown—would come to London, and we would put a band together and cut Johnny's new album in a few days. On occasion they would want to work in Paris. I took Jimmy Page over for one album, where he was nothing short of brilliant, and on another I recommended the Small Faces for the sessions, with the addition of Peter Frampton on guitar. Johnny would always pay cash, and the Small Faces jumped at the opportunity to take advantage of a few quid in the pocket and a couple of days in the French capital.

Sadly, they had a huge disagreement on the session that was never repaired, and that was that. Steve went off and formed Humble Pie with Peter Frampton, who I had known for some years through Bill

WITH THE SMALL FACES AT OLYMPIC STUDIOS. FROM LEFT:
STEVE MARRIOTT, ME, RONNIE LANE, IAN (MAC) McLAGAN.
KENNEY JONES ISN'T PICTURED.

Wyman and Peter's band The Herd; Greg Ridley, who I knew from working with Spooky Tooth in the sixties; and Jerry Shirley, who I had never met, but who at only seventeen years old proved to be a really good drummer and a very pleasant man.

Meanwhile, Ronnie Lane, Kenney Jones, and Ian McLagan got back to London and set about putting the Faces together with Ronnie Wood and Rod Stewart.

Both bands eventually asked me to produce them. Humble Pie was ready first, but I waited until they had a deal with A&M in 1970 and then I agreed to go into Olympic and make the album *Humble Pie* without even hearing them. This proved to be a bit of a mistake on my part, as although they were all really good musicians and pleasant enough to work with, Steve Marriott had changed musical horses and this band was loud, extremely energetic, using variations on the same riff, with very few good songs. They were popular enough, and became quite successful by working incredibly hard, constantly touring America. But they lacked the substance that I had hoped for, particularly knowing what Steve was capable of as a songwriter. So the experience was disappointing for me and after a second attempt with the album *Rock On* (not the most innovative album title), I decided to stop working with them.

I did not get to produce the Faces until their third album, *A Nod Is as Good as a Wink . . . to a Blind Horse*, in late 1971. It was good to get back in the studio with my pals Kenney, Ronnie, and Mac, and to meet Ronnie Wood for the first time. I had seen Rod around in the sixties and had always been a great admirer of his voice, but it was not until he joined the Faces that I really came to appreciate his skill as a vocalist. Their style of playing, coupled with the material they wrote, really suited him and showed him off to his best.

They were really easy to work with, all of us sharing a similar sense of humor. Ronnie Lane, Kenney, Mac, and I picking up where we left off with the Small Faces, with the addition of Woody's and Rod's personalities and musicianship bringing a whole new and fresh start. This was rough-and-ready rock and roll with a twinkle in its eye. The album went Top 10 in America, and we had a hit single with "Stay with Me."

By the time we got to the next album, *Ooh La La*, things had changed quite a bit. Rod was having huge success as a solo artist with his worldwide number-one "Maggie May," and his interest in the band was waning, with him showing less and less interest in the album we were making. The band had been hugely successful in its own right, but that was not enough to keep him. I think we were all pleased when the record was finished.

It was not long before they split up. It was inevitable, really. After the American tour to promote *Ooh La La*, Ronnie Lane was the first to leave the band. When he got back from the States, he rang to tell me the news. He was really depressed and at a bit of a loss as to know what to do. I asked him if he had any songs. He replied that he had a couple. So in order to cheer him up, I suggested that we go into Olympic later that week and record them, as I had a couple of days free. This resulted in the single "How Come?" becoming a number one in the UK for Ronnie when it was released a few weeks later. That cheered him up a bit. The rhythm section I put together that day— Benny Gallagher, Graham Lyle, and Bruce Rowlands, along with the fiddle player Charlie Hart—ended up staying with Ronnie, and became his band, Slim Chance, adding the ever faithful and unbelievably competent Russell Schlagbaum as manager, road manager, and problem solver extraordinaire. They went on the road around the UK, using a circus tent as a portable venue.

Kenney Jones, certainly one of the best drummers of the era, has kindly played on many sessions with other artists for me and went on to replace Keith Moon in The Who. He lives close by and remains a valued friend today. Ian McLagan moved on after the Faces to play with the Stones, Bonnie Raitt, and Bob Dylan, among many others. He now lives in Austin, Texas, where he has a successful solo career. We are still good pals, and I had the pleasure of mixing his last two solo albums. We all know what happened to Woody—he joined the Stones not long after I quit.

The Small Faces, along with the Faces, finally got the recognition they deserve in America, being inducted into the Rock and Roll Hall of Fame in 2012.

Ronnie Wood, Pete & Eric, the "Black Box" Album, and the Last Meeting with John, 1971

In 1971, I started to look for a larger house to live in, before the birth of my second child, Abigail. A friend of my mother's had a beautiful late-nineteenth-century house with seven bedrooms and a large, well-established garden. It had been the lodge to the Tattenham Estate on the edge of the Epsom racecourse, not far from where we were already living. It was the perfect family home and really well situated. London was only twenty miles to the north, and to the south we were bordered by woodland that led to open countryside all the way to the coast some forty miles away. He was anxious to sell. So as there was no agent involved and I knew him well, we were able to negotiate a really good deal relatively quickly.

I was feeling pretty pleased with myself and had completed the purchase the week before, when at around three a.m. at the end of a session with the Faces, Woody announced that he had been given the keys that afternoon to a house he had bought from the actor John Mills. He asked if I would like to accompany him on his first visit as the new owner. I jumped at the opportunity, being nosy and wanting to see how his purchase stacked up against mine.

It was a short drive west from Olympic along the river and up to the top of Richmond Hill. The house was very grand and impressive from the outside. We parked up, and Woody produced a bunch of keys, none of which worked in the lock. Not to be beaten, he decided to break in. I was not sure that that was a good idea, particularly the way we looked. Two fairly unkempt guys at three a.m., breaking in to a house that everyone locally would have known belonged to the famous actor.

Fortunately there was no alarm. We gingerly entered and found the light switch in the hall that revealed a grand room with the classic black-and-white squares of marble floor so often used in eighteenth-century houses and a beautifully proportioned staircase. Woody, leading the way, proceeded to show me round. It was without a doubt the most beautiful house I had ever been in. Quite breathtaking.

It was on four floors, the main feature being three large oval rooms one on top of the other, all with stunning understated ornate ceilings. On the ground floor was the drawing room, above was the master bedroom, and below was the dining room. Even the doors were slightly curved to complete the perfect oval. In the basement were a huge kitchen and an oak-paneled snooker room with the most beautiful table, which had once been owned by the world champion Joe Davis.

There was a conservatory on the ground floor that had the most fantastic view of the River Thames winding away to the west, and from a bedroom on the top floor at the front of the house was a panoramic view of the rooftops of London to the east. I remember Woody announcing with lecherous glee that we were standing in Hayley's room—John Mills's actress daughter, who, apparently, he had spent his youth fantasizing about.

When I found out that he had paid only a little more than I had for my new place, I have to admit I was extremely jealous. He soon put in a small studio on the lower ground floor. That room was where the basic track for the Stones' "It's Only Rock 'n Roll (But I Like It)" was cut. With Kenney Jones playing the drums. Charlie was not deliberately left out. Mick and Keith went round to Woody's place for a jam and Kenney happened to be there. It turned out so well that they ended up using it.

There was a fabulous cottage at the end of the steeply sloped garden that Ronnie Lane lived in for a while, and after him the next tenant was Keith Richards.

Pete Townshend called me one day in December 1972, telling me that he was really worried about Eric Clapton, as he had become a heroin-induced recluse along with his girlfriend, Alice. Pete felt that he had to get Eric out playing again. So he put together a wonderful rhythm section with Ronnie Wood, Jim Capaldi, Steve Winwood, Rick Grech, Rebob, and Jimmy Karstein, and had Robert Stigwood book the Rainbow in London a few weeks later for one night only, and asked if I could help with the rehearsals and record the show. So as Woody and I were in the middle of the Faces album *Ooh La La*, we took a week off. Woody generously offered his house for rehearsals, and Ronnie Lane donated his Airstream mobile recording unit to record it.

I was keen to do all I could to help but had little faith in Eric even turning up. Which he eventually did. At this point I was not a big fan, but that was based on his use of heroin and what it did to his personality and his ability to play. I have yet to meet a heroin addict that I would choose to have any kind of social intercourse with let alone a creative relationship, and I am sure the feeling would be mutual.

They got through the show with the band carrying Eric as best they could. His performance was less than sparkling. Understandable really, as he was not in good shape. It was suggested that he should come to Olympic a few days later to replace some of the weaker performances. So when Eric did not show for the overdub session, I said I would not mix the album as it stood, as it would certainly not be in Eric's best interest for it to be released without it being tidied up. Robert Stigwood, who was managing Eric at the time, was really keen to have an album to put out. So he got Bob Pridden to mix it as it was, who I am sure did a great job but it seemed that Mr. Stigwood had little or no concern for the integrity of his artist.

God knows what Pete's action saved Eric from. It certainly got him motivated to join the real world again and to start playing. Perhaps he saved his life.

Once Woody and his first wife, Krissy, had settled into their new home, it became a great place to hang out. They were always pleased to see you and encouraged friends to call in if they were in the area. It was on one such afternoon's visit in November 1974 that we were joined in the kitchen by Mick Jagger. He and I had been to see the Faces play in London not long before, where they had put on a formidable show that had impressed him mightily.

He explained to me over a cup of tea that the Stones were in something of a quandary. They were in the process of extricating themselves from their deal with Allen Klein and it turned out that they owed him one more album under the terms of their contract. So the band had decided to go through all the recordings they had made during the term of the contract and find material that had been rejected for one reason or another and assemble it into an album to satisfy the legal requirements of the deal.

Although I had stopped working with the Stones sometime before, I had recorded all the material that they were considering using, so Mick, and I presume Keith, had decided to ask me to briefly return to the fold and go to New York for a few days in order to put together what became known as the "Black Box" album. As I was free later that week, I was happy to oblige.

On the plane on the way over, I remember Mick leaving his seat next to me and going to chat with an extremely well-dressed elderly gentleman for at least half an hour who I think was the Lord Chief Justice of the day. How quickly things had changed. It seemed only five minutes ago that the whole of the establishment in England was bitterly against what The Rolling Stones stood for, locking them up and making examples of them, and here we were at thirty-five thousand feet, with Mick engaged in charming social repartee with one of the lawmakers of the land.

Over the next few days we got on with the job in hand, going through hours of multitrack tapes. There was a very good reason why this material had not been included on any album before. It was almost entirely unfinished ideas that had come to nothing.

I must say I enjoyed the time with Mick. Although we had known each other for years, it was rare for us to spend a concerted amount of time together without the circus that surrounds the band.

We went for a drink one night in the bar of the hotel and he asked if I would consider going back to work with them. We had had this conversation many times before and it had usually turned quite ugly, with me maintaining that I had put my time in as their engineer and was only prepared to continue with them if they recognized me as a producer and gave me a royalty, and with him refusing to give me a royalty and calling me, among other things, a whore.

Though I had been producing with some degree of success for some time, Mick and Keith only ever saw me as an engineer. Their process seemed to be getting slower and slower. The flush of Mick Taylor joining the band had subsided somewhat. Substance abuse had changed him almost beyond recognition from the quiet fresh-faced genius I met when he joined the band.

In fact, the last time I had worked for the Stones was in 1972, re-cording and mixing some of *Exile on Main St.* My brother Andy did most of the album at Keith's house in the South of France, where, sadly, he fell under the spell of Keith and heroin. Things had not gone particularly well as a result of a massive amount of drug taking by everyone except Mick, Charlie, and Bill. So Mick invited me down to visit, and not long after, he asked if I would go in with him on his own to help him finish a couple of vocals and do some mixing. My one condition was that it would only be him and me, with no inter-ference from any other member of the band, after what I had wit-nessed in France.

We started back in London at Basing Street Studios and were getting on really well, slipping straight back right where we left off. Until, on the second day, the control room door opened and much to my surprise in walked Mick Taylor. We had been working on a mix for about half an hour and had discovered that Mick Taylor had over-dubbed himself on drums and bass and was singing background parts, all of which I had decided not to use, as The Rolling Stones al-ready had the best rhythm section that I knew of and I would not insult them by using what he had played as a substitute in the mix. As for the singing, I felt it would be best if he stuck to playing the guitar. On realizing that I was only using his guitar part, Mr. Taylor became quite upset and demanded to know where his bass, drums, and singing were. I politely explained that they would be remaining on the multitrack tape and that I would not be using them in the mix, as I felt they added nothing of value to the track. This was a changed man. He had become an insufferable egomaniac. I reminded Mick Jagger of our agreement, and he asked Mick Taylor to leave, agreeing with me that having him there was not going to work. That was the last time I saw him, until I did a live album with Bob Dylan ten years later, in 1984. He was in the band and had straightened himself out and reverted back to being the quiet, unassuming guy I had once known.

That session was the last time that Mick and I had the conversation about me going back to work with the Stones and I declined. After a couple of drinks in the bar in New York, I agreed on the condition that I would co-produce with him and Keith.

The next day, as the session was finishing, Mick announced that he was going to spend the evening with John Lennon at his place and asked if I would like to come along. Some months prior to this, John had been interviewed by one of the English tabloids about the *Let It Be* album, and for some unknown reason to me, had chosen to slag me off in an extremely unpleasant way. So I declined the invitation, telling Mick the reason why. He told me I was being ridiculous, and after much discussion, persuaded me to come along, making me promise to be on my best behavior and not challenge John about what he had said in the press.

We arrived at John's apartment and to my surprise, I was greeted with much affection. He was living with May Pang. Yoko had arranged for her to be with him while she was away. We spent a pleasant evening watching TV and chatting.

When it came time to leave, I felt it would be hypocritical of me to go without mentioning the article in the press and John's extraordinary venom aimed at me over the *Let It Be* sessions. So, as we got to the front door to leave, I turned and, in as pleasant a way possible, asked him if he could explain himself, since he had appeared to be so pleased to see me and yet had been extraordinarily unpleasant in the interview.

He turned to me and told me that he had been equally vicious about Paul during the same period and that Paul had got it right when he had declared that the only person John was hurting with his vitriolic behavior was himself. It was not exactly an apology, more like an explanation. This outpouring of negativity had taken place during John's "primal scream" period in Los Angeles, when apparently he came off the rails for a while. We parted company with a hug and a look of relief from Mick that I had not embarrassed him, having gone against my word to behave myself.

That was to be the last time I saw him. I am really glad that my last memory of John is such a pleasant one.

Black and Blue,
December 1974–
February 1975

Having come to an agreement with Mick in New York for me to return to the fold, a couple of weeks later I was on my way to Munich to start their next album. The day that we left for Germany, Mick Taylor announced that he was leaving the band. I can only assume that it was a dispute over the financial arrangement between him and the Stones. This turned out to be a bonus for me. Not because he would not be there, although I was not really looking forward to having to deal with what he had become, but because it was like going back to the beginning, the original team, only without Brian and with the addition of Nicky Hopkins. I must say I took great comfort in this and enjoyed the sessions immensely.

We got a huge amount done in the twelve days we were there. In fact, I thought we had very nearly finished the record. My favorite track from these sessions was "Fool to Cry." Mick played electric piano and delivered a brilliant vocal. I still have the rough mix I did in Munich the night we finished, having put a synthesized string section on with Nicky Hopkins, and I think it eats the version that they finally released a year later.

We reconvened on the 21st of January in Rotterdam. The Stones were trying to avoid paying tax in the UK so were intent on recording out of the country. Hence the sessions in Munich and now Rotterdam. Stu had found a concert orchestra rehearsal facility that he felt would be suitable to use as a studio, so we took the Stones Truck, parked it outside, and ran what seemed like several miles of cable into the building along endless corridors up to the second floor into a large room with a high ceiling and excellent acoustics for a symphony orchestra, but was not at all suitable for a rock and roll band. Still, we made the best of it.

After a few days, having made a fairly slow start, I got word that Little Feat was playing in Amsterdam and suggested that we should all go and see them, thinking it might be stimulating and give the band a bit of a kick into gear. The night before I left for Rotterdam, I went to a reception at the American Embassy in London that Warner Bros. had arranged in order to promote a tour round Europe with a bunch of American acts that they had recently signed. I attended because the band Little Feat was among them. I had been introduced to them in 1973 by David Anderle, who had sat me down at his house in L.A. and played me their album *Dixie Chicken*. This was an extraordinary group of musicians put together by their leader Lowell George and the keyboard player Billy Payne. Lowell was the singer and an unbelievable guitar player and Billy was nothing short of a genius on the piano. Add to this Richie Hayward on drums, Kenny

Gradney on bass, and Sam Clayton on percussion and you get the slipperiest southern/New Orleans rock and roll you ever heard. They had the same effect on me as Delaney & Bonnie did the first time I heard them. A new sound and completely brilliant musicianship.

So we all jumped into cabs and took the short drive to the venue in Amsterdam, turning up in the middle of their set. We were ushered into the wings by the promoter, where we were treated to one of the best live shows I have ever seen. They proved to be every bit as good as their album suggested. Maybe even better. We all stood there with our jaws on the floor as, one by one, the guys onstage realized who was standing in the wings. They had no idea we were coming and, having got over the shock, seemed to even kick it up another notch. Years later, Richie Hayward told me jokingly that he would never forgive me for stopping his heart that night, turning to see the entire Rolling Stones standing in the wings, watching their show.

My ploy did not have any visible effect on the Stones' sessions, particularly as Mick and Keith had decided to use them to audition guitar players to replace Mick Taylor. A huge amount of recording time was wasted, as over the next few days, a steady progression of hopeful guitarists from near and far trooped up and down the stairs and corridors of the building we were in. The sessions started later and later. This coupled with the fact that I was stuck out in the truck miles away from the little bit of action, if any, that was taking place each night. Things were slipping back to how it had been when I quit, and the speed and efficiency of the Munich sessions was left in the dust.

On the tenth day, after a falling out with Keith, the first and last I ever had, I quit in yet another puff of steam. A few hours later, on my way down to check out of the hotel, I called by Mick's room, at his request, to say a final farewell. He had left the door open and called to me to come into the bathroom, where we had our final conversation. We had been through all manner of trials and tribulations, having run the gamut of what enormous success had brought them. I had spent far more time with them than with my wife and kids and I had been privileged to witness the creation of some of the best rock and roll of the era, and it all ended with him in the bath and me standing in the doorway with my coat on and my suitcase at my feet. What a strange way to finish a working relationship that had started all those years ago in our youth.

On the rare occasion that we have met since, Keith has greeted me with warmth, the episode in Rotterdam long forgotten. Possibly our mutual unspoken grief for the loss of our friend Stu being the underlying factor.

In 2012, I mixed an album that Don Was and Keith produced in New York with Aaron Neville. The mix was done in London at British Grove and only Don was available to attend. This resulted in me getting a charming handwritten letter of thanks from Keith, which I was really touched by, it being a first in all those years. It will serve to remind me of the more positive aspect of my relationship with him and the band.

Thirty-five years after my last session with the Stones, Don Was asked me to mix a version of the two new tracks they recorded in Paris for the fiftieth-anniversary album. It was a lovely gesture on his part, and it was wonderful to have a momentary reunion. Mick and Keith came separately to supervise the mix of the song they had each written on their own, with Charlie and Ronnie Wood popping in for ten minutes to say hi. How things have changed. The tolerance that existed between Mick and Keith has long since dissipated, as they are unwilling to write together anymore, resulting in a somewhat watered-down "glimmer" of what the band was. However, many of my friends have seen them play live in the past few months and report back that they are as good as ever. How bad can that be after fifty years? As for me, I have no further desire to see them play, as I prefer to remember the band as it was with Stu and Bill.

WITH BILL WYMAN AND JIMMY MILLER BACKSTAGE
AT MEADOWLANDS, NJ, 1981.

Fairport Convention, Keith Moon, Derek Green, AFL, and Joan Armatrading

On returning to London from Rotterdam in 1975, I found I had no time to reflect on the abrupt end to the Stones era. I did a couple of days of preproduction with Georgie Fame and then immediately went on to the one and only album I got to make with Fairport Convention, *Rising for the Moon*. This was the first time I had worked with any of them and it proved to be a terrific experience and enormously beneficial to my future. The drummer Dave Mattacks and the guitar player Jerry Donahue bringing their finely honed and original talents to the many projects they worked on with me over the next few years. Sandy Denny proved to be every bit as good a singer as I suspected. The song "White Dress" from this album remains one of my all-time favorites. I suggested that the lovely Dave Pegg should take a bass solo, giving this egoless man a rare opportunity to be in the spotlight for a few seconds. The brilliant icon of the fiddle Dave Swarbrick supports beautifully on the viola, while Sandy gives a stunning vocal performance of one of the many songs she wrote.

Three years later, drugs and alcohol taking their toll, she fell and died from a head injury.

Next was The Who and the start of *The Who by Numbers*. We were working at Ramport, their studio in Battersea and had been trying to cut one song all day long. Keith was not in the best shape and found it difficult to remember the arrangement and made a mistake in each take. Everyone was very supportive and no one gave him a bad time, we just kept going. Trying all the tricks of coffee breaks, playing a different song for a while, then coming back to the original. All to no avail. In the end we took yet another break, as I didn't think anyone had another take in them.

Keith remained, sitting at his kit in the studio, looking somewhat dejected. I went out to try and cheer him up.

My encouragement fell on deaf ears. He was upset and felt he was letting the others down. So I suggested, in as pleasant a way as possible, that if he really felt that way then maybe to rectify the problem he should stop drinking for a few days and come to the sessions straight, to increase his attention span when trying to remember the more complicated arrangements he was confronted with. Our friendly chat immediately turned sour. "It is all very well for you to suggest that I stop drinking," he spat at me. "You must smoke sixty cigarettes a day, and have done ever since I have known you. What if I told you to stop smoking?" Okay, I told him. I will stop smoking if you stop drinking. "It's a deal," he said, visibly relaxing and shaking my hand.

I stopped smoking there and then, and of course, he made absolutely no attempt to stop drinking. So dear Keith may well have saved me from lung cancer and certain death, for all I know.

These sessions were followed by a request from Derek Green at A&M in London for me to make an album with Andy Fairweather Low. This also ended up being beneficial to me in several ways. We made a fabulous album, from which we had a hit single in the UK, "Wide Eyed and Legless." Perhaps most important of all, we became lifelong friends. He introduced me to the drummer Henry Spinetti and the amazing John "Rabbit" Bundrick, a frighteningly good keyboard player. Andy became my go-to rhythm guitar player on many albums for many years. He had been in the very successful band Amen Corner in the sixties. The album we made was his second as a solo artist, and I shall always be grateful to Derek for the introduction.

Derek Green was probably the most influential record company executive in Europe in the seventies. In 1972, he took the job of managing director of A&M Records in London at the ripe old age of twenty-seven, having been previously retained by Chuck Kaye in 1969 to set up and run A&M's publishing company Rondor Music in Europe.

His story is quite extraordinary. Having left school at age sixteen with his only interests being football and music, he got a job as a messenger at Carlin Music, a very successful music publisher in London. His only qualification being that he had a bike. They took him on at the recommendation of his girlfriend, who worked there and was fed up with getting stuck with the bill every time they went out together.

Being the type of guy that he is, he realized that the only way to get noticed and progress was to become the best messenger that one could possibly be. With his sights set on becoming a song plugger in the company's "professional department," his enthusiasm was quickly rewarded with a job in the sheet music department and then on to a royalty clerk, eventually making it to his objective, becoming a song plugger at age eighteen, a job he was extremely good at.

By the time he was twenty-four, having helped to establish subsidiary publishing companies for Strike Records and RCA in London, he was an obvious choice for Jerry Moss and Chuck Kaye at A&M in Los Angeles to help them get their publishing foot in the door in Europe. Among the artists he signed were Yes, Albert Hammond, Johnny Nash, and Bob Marley. So when the position of managing director for the label in Europe became vacant, he was the obvious choice. He was reluctant to accept, as his heart was in publishing, but thankfully for all involved he was persuaded by Abe Somer to take the job.

In the next few years he established the label as an independent in Europe, and with the help of Mike Noble as head of A&R and the team he set up around him, Derek signed and guided some of the most influential British artists in the popular music of the day, while retaining the originality and ethos of the parent label in America. These included the platinum-selling artists Supertramp, The Police, Peter Frampton, Humble Pie, Joan Armatrading, Rick Wakeman, Sting, Stealers Wheel, Chris de Burgh, Squeeze, Joe Jackson, Elkie Brooks, and Gallagher & Lyle.

He spotted and signed the Sex Pistols, albeit a short-lived triumph, as before the ink was dry on the contract he became disenchanted with their violent behavior. They physically assaulted the disc jockey Bob Harris at a club in London's West End and, after a press conference to announce their signing, turned up and wrecked A&M's offices on New King's Road. Although he still believed in their music, he felt that he could not sanction their behavior and was forced to drop them like a hot potato. So he should be credited with being one of the first to recognize the commercial viability of punk, which was very much against the grain of the rest of the industry at that time, and something that I shall never thank him for.

My first encounter with him was not a pleasant one. I had just delivered *Willie and the Lapdog*, an album I am terribly proud of, that I produced for A&M with Gallagher & Lyle. These two had been the writers in McGuinness Flint and had left the band to establish themselves on their own, asking me to continue with them as their producer. They were wonderful songwriters, appealing to my folk roots, and a refreshing contrast to the rock and roll I had been immersed in for so long.

Graham Lyle telephoned me to say that the newly installed head of the company in London had refused their request for a booklet of lyrics to be inserted in the sleeve of their album, on the grounds that it would be too expensive. As he was getting nowhere, he asked if I could take over and have a crack at persuading Derek to change his mind. Not knowing Derek at all, I foolishly assumed that he was just another egotistical, jumped-up record company executive. So when he took my call, I ripped into him, accusing him of being cheap and disrespectful to my artist, neither adjective normally being associated with A&M. In fact, it was me who was being disrespectful and incredibly rude. Derek dealt with my bullying outburst in the most diplomatic way, without rising to the bait, remaining calm and polite. So by the end of the conversation, without me even realizing, he had my respect and it is to his credit and the fact that he gave in to our request that we remain close friends to this day.

While at A&M he used his relationships with various DJs from his song-plugging days to great effect and employed a team of like-minded individuals from a similar background to him to promote the label's product with wonderful success.

After twelve years with A&M, he moved on to start his own label, China Records, and, with Bob Grace, the publishing company Empire Music. Both companies achieved equal success, eventually being sold to Warner Bros. and PolyGram Music, respectively.

Perhaps his finest achievement is what he gave back to the business with his time on the board of the BPI, the association that represents the British Phonographic Industry, and his time as chairman of the board of Nordoff-Robbins Music Therapy, the charity that is supported by the music business. He was the driving force behind a concert at Knebworth that raised the money to buy the charity its headquarters and to fund the building of the BRIT School, a school for the performing arts in South London that he served invaluably on the Board of Governors in its infancy. This school is the first of its kind in Britain—a state school that is funded annually by the music business and gives kids from all walks of life an opportunity for free education in music, dance, and drama.

Derek is an extraordinary man, who never lost sight of where he came from, bringing his exceptional taste and business acumen to all he encountered.

Having finished recording with Andy, I went back in with The Who to complete *The Who by Numbers* at Shepperton Studios. They had bought a soundstage there, and we used the Stones Truck once more to finish the recording, ending up at Basing Street to mix.

As I had to return to L.A. once more to master the album at Doug

Sax's Mastering Lab, I decided to take the family and have a working holiday. So I rented a house on Coldwater Canyon in Beverly Hills for the month of August to use as a base.

I was still married to my first wife, Sylvia. We had two children— a son, Ethan, and a daughter, Abigail. John Entwistle called and asked if he could come by with his wife, Alison, and their son, Christopher, so that the kids could play together. So we invited them over for lunch and were having a drink while the children played happily outside around the pool when the doorbell rang, and much to my surprise there stood Keith Moon, immaculately dressed in a white suit. John was visiting L.A. for a few days and had invited him, thinking it would be okay with me, and had forgotten to mention it. Keith was living there at that point, so he saw it as an opportunity to kill two birds with one stone and see us both together.

He joined the party and all was going well until the gardeners turned up and started to water all the plants around the pool area. We brought the children inside out of the way, leaving their clothes and toys by the pool. I went back to get their things only to find that they had been liberally watered by the gardeners. I mentioned this to John, apologizing for their carelessness. The house was a typical California design with a very large open-plan area opening out onto a paved terrace, beyond which was the pool. As John and I stood there in conversation, we were interrupted by a loud Tarzan-like holler. Keith, having stripped to his underpants, launched himself from the back of the room and ran at full speed through the house onto the terrace and threw himself into the pool, taking the two poor unsuspecting gardeners with him. The older man could not swim and I dived in to help pull him out. Both he and what turned out to be his son were visibly shaken and had no more idea than me why they had been knocked into the pool. I apologized profusely but as I did not speak Spanish it fell on deaf ears, and they left drenched to the skin, never to return. Keith muttered something about teaching them a lesson for watering the kid's things and disappeared into the house to dry himself off, having been asked to leave by me.

John and I had made arrangements to go to Fred Walecki's music store in Westwood for John to look at the new Alembic bass guitar. So we hopped in the car, leaving Alison and Christopher at the house, and thinking that Keith was leaving, left for Fred's. Once we had gone Keith reappeared, only to be confronted by my wife, who admonished him for what he had done, saying how awful it was for those poor men to have to drive home in wet clothes. When Keith showed no concern for their predicament, she took the immaculate white suit he had arrived in and deposited it in the pool, saying, "Well, perhaps you would like the same experience." He apparently went berserk for a few minutes, and having calmed down, persuaded Sylvia to lend him a white kaftan with a floral motif embroidered on the front, which he duly put on and left, still complaining about the wet cash in the pocket of his suit.

A couple of months after my tenure at the house, I received a bill for several thousand dollars from the owner. The gardeners required new watches and had quite understandably never returned, so when I left, as the house was unattended, all the plants had died and the entire garden had to be replanted.

Many years later, Eric Clapton and I were swapping stories about The Who when he told me that one afternoon in August 1975, Keith had inexplicably turned up where he was staying at the Hyatt House hotel on Sunset Boulevard in Los Angeles, wearing a white dress with a floral motif embroidered on the front.

There are many stories about Keith Moon's extraordinary behavior, most of which sound amusing when told. In reality, these incidents were anything but funny to witness, as they very often involved some degree of violence or destruction of someone else's property. He *was* capable of being very funny. Unfortunately, it very rarely stopped there, and what started out being amusing ended up being extremely unpleasant.

Then it was off to Tulsa, Oklahoma, to finish the Georgie Fame album with Jamie Oldaker on drums and Carl Radle on bass. I had been a huge fan of Carl's for years, so working with him was a thrill, and a massive learning experience for me. We finished up back in L.A. to mix and master it. While there I had a meeting with Chuck Kaye on the lot at A&M. He had recently been made head of A&R as well as running the company's publishing company, Almo. I have always had a huge respect for Chuck. He epitomized the best of the music business at this point in time. He was a warm and friendly character with a wonderful sense of humor, great taste in music and in no way full of his own self-importance like so many of his counterparts. He was a good friend to me, offering some wonderful advice over the years, for which I shall always be grateful. So when he asked me to go and check out an artist on A&M with the view of me producing her, I was happy to oblige and flew with him to Washington, D.C., to see her play at the Cellar Door club.

I remember it was a very small stage with a very large band crammed onto it. The singer was painfully shy, barely lifting her head from her chest to look at the audience, and mumbling incoherently in between songs. The sound was not at all good and she was overpowered by the band. So, thanking Chuck for the opportunity, I said it was not for me and returned home to England the next day.

Chuck, feeling that I had not seen the artist in circumstances that did her justice, called Derek Green, whose idea it had been to get me to produce her in the first place. They both called to let me know that they felt I was making a mistake, persuading me to take another listen. I suggested that we meet up in Derek's office in London, where she could play me a couple of songs on acoustic guitar, face-to-face, and thank God that I did, as the artist was Joan Armatrading.

I got it within the first few bars. By the time she had finished I could not believe how I could have misjudged the extraordinary talent that was sitting opposite me. Not only did she have the most wonderful voice, but the songs and her delivery of them were so original, and she was one of the best rhythm guitarists I have ever heard.

So once again, I very nearly missed out on one of the finest talents I have ever had the good fortune to work with, and it was only through the perseverance of others that I started work on the *Joan Armatrading* album three weeks later at Olympic Studios. I assembled the finest musicians I knew, knowing that they all would have to be pretty hot to keep up with her: Dave Markee on bass; Dave Mattacks, Kenney Jones, and Henry Spinetti on drums; Jerry Donahue, electric guitar; and at Derek's recommendation, Tim Hinkley on piano. They all complemented Joan and her music with great skill. She was still painfully shy in the studio, finding it difficult to communicate with the musicians directly, addressing any comments she had through me to them. We cut her first hit in the UK, "Love and Affection," on these sessions, with Brian Rogers picking up on Dave Markee's melodic bass line and shadowing it with his string arrangement, and Joan brilliantly coming up with the idea to use the bass voice for the first line of the chorus on what was already a fabulous track. What a song and what a vocal performance.

This was yet another occasion when I felt like I was involved with something very special being introduced through someone else's talent to a new music experience, coming to realize that not only did I relate to it but finding that I could contribute in some small way to the proceedings. The excitement this brings is completely consuming.

We had weekends off while we were making the album and I would spend them playing back what we had done, on my own or with anyone I could muster, being so excited by what we had achieved in the previous few days.

I became very protective of Joan, so when she appeared a few weeks later at Hammersmith Odeon in London and then at the Lincoln Center in New York to promote the record, I went along to take care of the sound in the auditorium just to make sure she would be represented in the best light possible after my experience of seeing her in Washington. All she needed in order for her extraordinary talent to be recognized was a really good band and a sound that did her justice.

Having worked with the bass player Bryan Garofalo and the drummer David Kemper in L.A. with Bernie Leadon, I recommended them to Joan the following year for her next album, *Show Some Emotion*, adding Georgie Fame and Rabbit on keyboards and keeping Jerry Donahue on guitar. This record includes my other favorite song of Joan's, "Willow," which has another sympathetic string arrangement by Brian Rogers and a remarkable vocal performance from Joan.

I have very fond memories of these first two albums that I made with Joan. They are up there with my favorites from all the records I have made.

Rough Mix and
Slowhand, 1976–77

In the late summer of 1976, Ronnie Lane went to see Pete Townshend to ask for help, as he was in some financial difficulty. Pete suggested that the best way he could assist was for them to make an album together. They telephoned me from the meeting to put the idea to me and asked if I would be willing to get involved as an equal partner in the project. I had been really good friends and worked with both of them for years, so it was a no-brainer. My only condition was that, as the idea had been inspired by Ronnie's need for money, they must both agree to take the project seriously and make the best album they could and not just do it for the cash. I was fascinated by the idea, as it was not an obvious musical pairing, and having been assured by both of them that they would treat it seriously, I agreed and we set about planning what was to become one of my favorite albums, and certainly one of the best that I ever made.

The idea was for there to be an equal split of material from each guy, with one supporting the other where possible. I remember quite clearly Pete coming to my house in Surrey, sitting on the couch, and playing me a song he had just written called "Street in the City." He had a D'Angelico archtop acoustic guitar that had the most extraordinary sound, particularly when he played it. I sat there transformed, feeling privileged to be there for this one-to-one performance by one of the best songwriters of our generation. As the song unfolded, it came to me that the only way to cut it and to do it justice was with Pete on his own with a huge string section. As the last chord drifted away I excitedly put the idea to him and he suggested that he approach his father in-law Ted Astley to do the arrangement. Ted was a well-known composer, mostly for TV movies, his most famous work being the theme for the British series *The Saint*. The three of us got together to discuss the idea, and a more charming and gentle man you could not wish to meet. My only input was to suggest that we use a really large section, as I wanted it to sound like the strings from a symphony orchestra. So we agreed on sixty strings.

When it came to the session, I sat Pete right in the middle of the orchestra so that he could play while having the extraordinary physical and emotive experience that being surrounded by all those harmonics provides. I truly believe that he had the same effect on them as they did on him. This was one of the most thrilling sessions I ever produced. The arrangement that Ted did was quite superb, with both Pete and the orchestra rising to the occasion, quite literally, as all sixty of them rose to their feet to applaud both Ted and Pete as we finished the take that was to be the master.

The rest of the material was cut in a more conventional way with a rhythm section. Charlie Watts played on the opening track, "My Baby Gives It Away," responding to the drive and fire of Pete's guitar with equal energy. For the rest of the record, we were fortunate to have the extraordinary skills of Henry Spinetti on drums. Apart from his amazing feel and technical ability he gets the most wonderful sound out of his kit, and I can think of no occasion when he ever came close to letting me down. I got Dave Markee to come and play upright bass on a couple of tracks. Dave and Henry were my stalwart rhythm section in England for years. Stu and John Bundrick, or "Rabbit" as he is better known, provided the keyboards.

Pete had written an instrumental for guitar. He told me that he wanted Eric Clapton to come and play it for the record. I thought this was a terrible idea as I felt that Pete should play his own instrumental; after all, it was his album. I had little time for Eric after the debacle of his concert and his not showing up at the studio to fix his performance. I thought that we could do without the negative energy that I associated with him at that time. Pete insisted and told me in no uncertain terms that there was no conversation. He was not going to play it and Eric was, as he had written it specifically for him.

I agreed, as it seemed that I had no option. I figured I could put up with the rather sour presence of Eric for an afternoon.

Well, I could not have been more wrong. We started the session at 2:30 p.m. Eric was on time and learned the piece really quickly and we had the track finished in no time. The whole experience being totally different than I had predicted. He was together and perfectly pleasant to work with.

A few days later he swung by the studio to see how we were doing. We had just finished a song called "April Fool." Ronnie had done a wonderful vocal, Dave Markee had come in and put a bowed double bass on it, and all we had left to do was the solo. We all thought a Dobro would be a great sound to complement what we had done, and Eric offered to play it.

There are a few moments in my recording career that I treasure and this is one of them. I played him the track and I noticed that his foot was tapping as he ran through the song. I quickly put a mic on his foot and we recorded the next run-through. It was note-perfect and quite beautiful. Eric reacting in the most natural and emotive way to the song and Ronnie's performance of it. Up until that moment I had paid very little attention to Eric as a musician and therefore never really understood what all the fuss was about. I thought he was just another bloody white kid playing the blues. That was very clearly my loss. In a matter of a few minutes I had been completely won over. This was a perfect example of what I have always thought since about Eric's playing. He never allows his brain to get in the way between his heart and his fingers.

He continued to visit us most days until we finished, and on the last day of recording he asked me if I would consider producing his next record. I said yes immediately, having been converted by the experience of the previous few days.

I shall be eternally grateful to Pete for insisting on using Eric on the album. There is still an enormous portion of boot in my mouth as a result of my unbelievably blinkered, opinionated, and intolerant attitude.

So, by a huge chunk of luck, I found myself going to see Eric Clapton play at the Hammersmith Odeon in London. It was the last date of his tour. I got back to England just in time, as when I had finished with Pete and Ronnie a month earlier, I went to L.A. and made an album with Bernie Leadon. He had left the Eagles and, having bought Neil Young's house in Topanga with a studio in the basement, had decided to make a record with his pal Michael Georgiades. It was a challenging environment to work in as the space was pretty tight, but we had a great time and made a very laid-back record.

Eric had asked me to the concert at Hammersmith to see if I agreed with the idea of using his current band for the record. The band turned out to be the perfect complement to where Eric was at musically at that time. I knew Dick Sims and Carl Radle, they were from Tulsa and had been introduced to me by Leon Russell. Add Jamie Oldaker to the mix, and a better rhythm section you could not wish for. The rest I did not know and the only member I did not think was necessary was the rather eccentric percussionist, who I am sure was really in the band for visual effect, as he seemed to contribute far more to the eye than to the ear by hurling himself round the stage like someone possessed.

The first session for *Slowhand* was on May 2nd at two-thirty p.m. By five p.m., we had our first track finished, and what a track it was. "Wonderful Tonight," this being the second song I had recorded that had been written for the gorgeous Pattie Boyd. I remember going home that night an extremely happy man. It was like falling off a log working with this lot. The rest of the record went as smoothly, with everyone seeming to enjoy the experience. Because they had been on the road for a few weeks, Eric and the band were in great form. There was a camaraderie between them socially as well as musically, Eric's sense of humor leading the way.

Eric was quite lazy in those days, and it was quite difficult to motivate him to work. However, once you had virtually dragged him into the studio, sat him down and thrust a guitar into his hands and told him to get on with it and play, all the aggravation dissipated. With his skill and the quality of the other musicians in the band, nothing took very long to cut. I would always record the first run-through, as something exceptional was bound to happen that would not be repeated in later takes.

I had a bit of a reputation as a disciplinarian and was quite strict about timekeeping. Much to our amusement, one evening Eric showed up at the studio with a note from Pattie, informing me that it was her fault and not Eric's that he was late. Just as a mother might write to her child's teacher.

Eric and I both being huge JJ Cale fans had a great time cutting "Cocaine." That led to the penning of "Lay Down Sally" by Marcy Levy, Eric, and George Terry, the rhythm guitar player in the band. This is of course a complete JJ Cale rip-off. Although these two tracks were very successful hit singles and I love them both, one of my favorites on the album is the John Martyn song "May You Never." I think it is the ease with which Eric sings it that I like so much, and the simplicity of the melody. His voice has become much stronger over the years since then, along with the fact that he had his broken nose fixed, which eliminated the slight nasal whine that was always present back in the days that I worked with him.

We were close to finishing the album when one evening we were visited by Lonnie Donegan, the man who started it all for so many of us. He sat in the control room with me for the rest of the session and as we were preparing to leave for home he asked if I would produce his next album. I am quite sure that he had no idea that I was the humble tape op on his sessions all those years ago at IBC and that he had the most extraordinary influence on my musical taste in my early teens. Although he was probably not in the least bit surprised when I told him, as so many of my contemporaries had done before. It was an amazing moment for me. It was as if I had gone the complete circle. Unfortunately I was unable to take him up on his request as I was already committed to another project during the time he had scheduled.

There are only nine tracks on the record. The reason being there were no more to be had. No one seemed to mind at the time, although I have always believed in using eleven or twelve. It is only fair to the punter who has forked out his or her hard-earned cash. Today this does not apply, as very few people listen to an album as a piece of work anymore. It is all about individual tracks being downloaded, and the label always wants to put on bonus tracks, without any thought to the flow of the album.

As a result of us working together on *Slowhand*, Eric and I became really good pals. We lived quite close to each other on the Surrey-Sussex border, and as my brother Andy had been married to one of Pattie's sisters, we even had a vague family connection. The friendship and the working relationship was to last for some years, until Eric made the decision to go straight and he stopped any contact with the large group of the friends that he'd associated with in his past to enable him to deal with the immense effort that it must have taken to become sober. He did not single me out and I never took it personally. I was selfishly disappointed, in that it seemed that I had lost a great friend, having been thrown out with the bathwater, so to speak. As time goes by I do hope we will reconnect, as I really miss him as a pal.

White Mansions and
The Legend of
Jesse James, 1978–79

O ne morning, I received in the mail a beautifully presented folder of lyrics and demos with a handwritten letter of introduction from an Englishman named Paul Kennerley. It was a project that he had written about the American Civil War. He had researched the war and written a collection of songs with lyrics full of accurate historical detail from the point of view of the South. I was most impressed, and at the first opportunity, arranged a meeting where I suggested that he develop the project by establishing different characters to tell the story. I thought it was an exceptional piece of work and was fascinated by the challenge of doing a concept album based on historical fact, although the characters he created to tell the story were fictitious. It turned out to be a surprisingly emotive subject.

Paul had been educated in the best schools in the land. As a result, he spoke with a perfect English accent, cutting quite a dash, being very tall and always immaculately dressed in his stiff collar and tie and Savile Row suits. However, he was obsessed with the American South, loved the Stones and country music, and when he sang, it was with the most exaggerated southern drawl, which to say the least, was somewhat disconcerting.

I took the idea to Derek Green. He was as impressed with Paul's work as I was and immediately signed him to a record and publishing deal. Once this had been agreed, we set about deciding who we could get to play and to sing the different roles that Paul had created. Jerry Moss, the M of A&M records, had a long-standing relationship with Waylon Jennings, so he managed to persuade him and his wife, Jessi Colter, to play the narrator and female lead, respectively. This was a massive coup for us, as they both added great credibility to the project.

I have always loved the "chemistry" part of my job, mixing up musicians who have not played together before, particularly Americans and British. So, having invited John Dillon and Steve Cash from The Ozark Mountain Daredevils to come and play and sing two of the roles, I put together my standby rhythm section of the day, Dave Markee on bass and Henry Spinetti on drums, adding Eric Clapton and Bernie Leadon to play guitars and Tim Hinkley for keyboards. We assembled in London, to make the record at Olympic Studios.

The demos that Paul had made in his basement at home were really inspiring, so playing them to everyone at the beginning of each session made my job so much easier. The sessions were a joy, everyone rose to the occasion. It would have been a rare experience for all this lot to come together and play, as it certainly was for me to produce. There can be a remarkable camaraderie that exists between those working on a project, and this was a classic case of that, everyone contributing with equal energy and intent to create something special and with each bringing out the best in the others.

Derek Green and Jerry Moss both believed in the project as much as we all did and were an integral part of the process of making the record. This made it all the harder for us all when it did not achieve the success we believed it deserved. It was unusual for me to have the label so involved while making a record, as I normally preferred to be left to my own devices, but on this occasion it proved to be a huge benefit and a good lesson learned.

The conventional process of promoting an album did not apply. Unfortunately, there was no obvious single to get radio play, and Jerry had a problem getting permission from Waylon's label to use anything featuring him for promotional purposes.

So we brought in Ethan Russell to shoot the album cover, and along with Mike Ross, the art director at A&M in London, created a book that went with the record. He took quite wonderful pictures that re-created the period and illustrated the characters and the drama of the story. So impressive was his work that A&M decided to promote the record by taking an audiovisual show on the road to major cities in the UK and America.

Everyone who took part was proud of the end result. It is sad that more people did not get to enjoy it. I think it is an outstanding piece of work by Paul Kennerley, and the performances from the artists did him credit, and it would seem that the few people who did get to hear it certainly agree.

There had been some delay between Paul's coming to me with *White Mansions* and our making the record. This was entirely my fault, as I was extremely busy at the time, and it was only as a

RECORDING *WHITE MANSIONS* AT OLYMPIC. FROM LEFT:
JOHN DILLON, STEVE CASH, WAYLON JENNINGS, ME.

WHITE MANSIONS SESSION AT OLYMPIC. L TO R: JOHN DILLON,
ERIC CLAPTON, PAUL KENNERLEY, BERNIE LEADON (LOITERING
IN THE BACKGROUND), AND DAVE MARKEE.

result of Paul's patience that I eventually got to make the record. He had put this time to good use by writing his next epic, *The Legend of Jesse James*, which follows on historically from the Civil War, and he presented me with the first demos as we were finishing *White Mansions*. He had researched this with the same minute attention to historical fact, and after some considerable effort, we were able to convince a wonderful array of talent to appear on the record.

This time the characters were not fictitious. Paul took a minimum of artistic license in the dialogue but other than that the story itself was really accurate.

So we started the process all over again of deciding who we should get to play each character. Paul and I were big fans of The Band and decided fairly quickly that our first choice to play Jesse James would be Levon Helm. By this point in time, he had started his career as a movie actor, and we discovered that he was making a movie in southern Spain. So having made contact through his agent, we jumped on a plane with a cassette player and the demos, and met up with him for dinner after what had been a long day's shooting for him. Levon and I had first met in 1969 when I recorded The Band with Bob Dylan at the Isle of Wight Festival. The following year he had asked me to mix The Band's *Stage Fright* album. So we already had a good working relationship going. He just needed to be convinced that the songs were musically compatible with his taste and quite understandably was interested in who else we were going to get to take part. We had a great evening, and once he got over the shock of Paul's innate Englishness, which seemed so out of context with the subject matter, he fell in love with the idea.

Emmylou Harris was the obvious choice for the female lead of Jesse James's love interest, and she readily agreed to take part. Now we were on a roll.

Next we had to get someone for the part of Frank James, Jesse's brother. We figured we should aim for the top and came up with the idea of Johnny Cash. Contact was made and the idea pitched. He agreed to meet us to discuss the possibility, which was a lot further than I thought we would get. I suspect that Waylon Jennings and Emmylou Harris had tipped him off that we were okay. He was on tour and we were invited to meet him at a rodeo that he was playing in Cheyenne, Wyoming. Once again we jumped on a plane and turned up at the appointed time and place, both a little nervous to meet the great man. We went backstage after the show and he very politely told us that he was very tired and asked if we could meet him the next day at nine a.m. at his hotel. We said we would be happy to do that and knocked on the door to his suite at precisely nine the following morning. After a short wait, the door was answered by a bleary-eyed Mr. Cash in his dressing gown and pajamas. We were embarrassed at having woken him up, but he was charming and made light of the situation, saying it was his fault that he had overslept. He ushered us into one of several bedrooms off the main living room of the suite and asked if we would not mind waiting in there while he got dressed. We nervously sat down on a bed that we could just make out in the darkened room, feeling like two schoolboys waiting for a beating from their headmaster and thinking that our luck was out, as surely he was not going to be receptive to our project, having just been woken from a deep sleep after what was almost certainly a very late night. We sat nervously on the edge of the bed for some minutes and all of a sudden there was the sound of movement from the other side of the room as someone turned over in their sleep. We both leapt to our feet and exited into the hallway, falling over each other in an attempt to get out of the room before more embarrassment befell us. As we tumbled out into the hallway, we ran straight into Johnny, who, now fully dressed, apologized with a grin, seemingly unconcerned about the room's occupant, and invited us to join him and June for breakfast in the dining area of the suite.

There she was. The great June Carter, sitting at the breakfast table, made up to the nines, beautifully turned out for that time in the morning, and charming to boot. They both very quickly put us at ease, and we got straight down to business. June's main concern was the lyrics that her husband was going to sing, so they were scrutinized while we ordered breakfast and played him demos of the songs he would sing, while explaining all we knew about the project. He seemed very impressed with Paul's writing, and after we agreed to change a couple of mild cusswords in the lyric, we got the thumbs-up. We left the hotel feeling really pleased with ourselves. We had pulled it off against all the odds and, I am sure, with a little help from Waylon.

We got Rosanne Cash to play Jesse's mother, and Charlie Daniels and Albert Lee—the genius English guitar player—to be the other members of the gang. We even managed to get Rodney Crowell to come and sing a small part.

The band were as impressive as the singers, with Levon playing drums, Emory Gordy bass, Tim Gorman keyboards, Albert Lee and the amazing Jesse Ed Davis on electric guitars, and Bernie Leadon playing guitar and banjo. Charlie Daniels played a bit of fiddle and Nick De Caro did wonderful string arrangements and played accordion, while both Emmylou and Paul glued the whole thing together with wonderful rhythm acoustic guitars.

Brian Ahern's studio in Los Angeles was perfect for the project, and he made us feel most welcome. It was a big room with a wooden floor and a high ceiling. So I was able to set up a large rhythm section quite comfortably with plenty of room to spare. I shall never forget sitting next to Emmylou in the control room and hearing her sing in my ear for the first time. There is not a microphone invented that can reproduce the true sound of her voice. It is like nothing I have ever heard. She is one of the truly great singers. Completely without ego. Treats everyone around her with respect, concern, and kindness. The consummate professional. The first to arrive and the last to leave, and she sings like an angel. It is no wonder that Paul Kennerley fell head over heels in love with her on these sessions and married her not long after.

We did all of Levon's tracks with him singing and playing the drums live. The only vocal overdub he did was his duet with Emmylou. Paul and I had rented a house not too far from the studio while we were working on the album and Levon stayed with us. He was great company and I never tired of the wonderful anecdotes he would relate late into the evening with his Camel cigarette–induced, husky southern drawl.

Johnny Cash was unable to come to Los Angeles for the sessions so Paul and I went to Nashville to record him, having cut the tracks in L.A. It was a Sunday afternoon and he came to the studio on his way back from a hunting expedition, asking Paul and me if we would like a haunch of venison as he arrived.

We asked if it would be okay to take some photographs while we were working. He readily agreed, but we were made to wait while he sent home for his customary all-black outfit.

To work with him was, without a doubt, one of the great privileges of my career. He could not have been more professional or pleasant to deal with and was eager to do the best job possible. His voice really is quite remarkable. One of the songs he sings, "Six Gun Shooting," is up there with my favorite recordings.

The making of this record was a great adventure. It was a wonderfully conceived piece of work by Paul Kennerley, and all of the artists and musicians involved seemed to enjoy the process enormously, giving some outstanding performances. This and *White Mansions* were two records that got away. They never received the recognition they deserved, and in my view, they still hold water today and remain albums that I'm very proud to have been involved with.

MTV

During the sixties the record companies took full advantage of radio as the most effective and free method of promoting their product. All the labels had staff "pluggers," whose job it was to get records played on the air by any means. This usually relied on a personal relationship with the DJs, who in those days invariably did their own programming. As a result, human nature being what it is, bribery in various forms became commonplace.

By the time the seventies came along, radio began to change drastically. It became more corporate, with small independent stations being acquired and having a corporate strategy applied to the way they operated, taking away their individuality, removing control of what was played and when to one central authority, and using what was called "psychographics." The playlist became a science. Music was segregated into boxes. The demographics of what age group and sex would be listening at any given time of the day were formulated, and music that was likely to appeal was programmed to suit. If your record did not fit into one of the prescribed boxes it would not be considered for airtime. So like an insidious disease, radio slowly began to dictate the types of records that were made, as we were constantly being told that in order to get airtime we had to produce to a predescribed menu. I found this to be most unsettling, considering it to be "the tail wagging the dog." It is fair to say that we had the benefit of free promotion for years with radio stations happy to ride on the back of the innovation that had taken place in popular music in the previous decade, but this had come about largely through the input of creative individuals operating with little or no restriction. This produced an environment that encouraged and applauded originality. What was happening to radio in the seventies threw a damp cloth on all of that, and what followed became more and more formulated to fit in a box.

Radio had a stranglehold on the record business that was relaxed only slightly by the advent of MTV in August 1981. All of a sudden, labels could reach the youth of America through cable TV. This was welcomed with open arms as a vibrant new way of promoting music. The new art form of the music video was created, giving many young aspiring moviemakers an opportunity to show off their skills, Ethan Russell leading the charge.

It was not long before the record companies were spending more on the video than on the production of the record it was promoting. This was fine if it worked and the record was a huge hit, but all too often the eventual sales did not justify this expense, putting pressure on the artists' viability as a commercial entity in the eyes of their label.

The constant battle to get product on the air eventually spawned a cynical exploiting of the young, with the marketing guys realizing that sexual titillation will get programmers to use their product. This resulted, unsurprisingly, in absolutely no self-censorship on the part of the music business.

The Clash,
1982

My working with The Clash came about through Steve Winwood's brother "Muff," the head of A&R for CBS in London at the time. He rang me in desperation, having finally taken delivery of the band's next album and it proving to be not quite what he had expected. Joe Strummer and Mick Jones would take it in turns to produce each album that they made but there had been some difference of opinion about this one and they had decided to book two separate studios in New York for two weeks and each do a complete mix of the album independently of the other. I am not sure who won, but what they had delivered to Muff did not pass muster in his opinion. So he called me to see if I could cast an unbiased ear on the record and, by remixing it, make it acceptable to all concerned.

If I am completely honest, I was not a fan of The Clash or, for that matter, any other punk band that existed. In fact, I had never really

ORIGINAL DOODLED ACETATE COVER FOR WHAT
BECAME *COMBAT ROCK*.

listened to them, but Muff was very convincing, and the fact that he had thought of calling me to help him out of his predicament intrigued me, as I had a great deal of respect for him.

He sent me two acetates of what turned out to be a double album. Someone, probably Joe Strummer, had drawn his version of a cartoon as artwork on the sleeve in thick felt-tip pen. I was quite skeptical as I went to listen, thinking that it would probably be an awful unmusical racket that I would not understand or have any sympathy with. Having listened to the whole thing, I got a pleasant surprise, and as self-indulgent as it was, I realized that they were really clever and that there was a great album to be had from what they had done. The combination of Joe's energy and intellect and Mick's musicianship was quite remarkable, along with Topper's excellent drumming. What attracted me as much as anything was their abundant sense of humor.

So having agreed to meet, they very kindly came down to my place in Sussex. I stepped outside to greet them as they arrived and the first very strange-looking guy got out of the car and introduced himself as Kosmo Vinyl. Not a good start. Kosmo had driven Joe and the band's manager, Bernie Rhodes, down to meet me. Mick Jones did not come; as it turned out, he was not interested in the whole idea.

It does show you how appearances can be deceptive. They turned out to be extremely polite and respectful. I hit it off with Joe straight away. The suggestions that I made about the record were readily accepted by him, so by the time the meeting was over I was even more intrigued and agreed to start immediately.

The tapes were delivered to the studio at my house in Warnham, and Joe came down from London for the bright and early start of ten a.m. I felt that some of the material was too long, so I set about editing some of the tracks in an effort to make them more concise. I felt the album would be a great deal stronger if it were a single rather than a double. All of these suggestions were greeted with much enthusiasm from Joe, which gave me the confidence to try any idea I had with regard to the sound or the arrangement of any song I was mixing. He encouraged me to be as avant-garde as possible and allowed me to change quite substantially the record that they had delivered to CBS a few days before.

At around seven p.m., the control room door opened and in walked a somewhat disgruntled Mick Jones. I welcomed him, sat him down and played him the mixes I had done that day. He sat unmoved, and when asked how he felt about what he had just heard, said he had several changes that he would like to make to each of them. I politely informed him that that was a shame as I had finished them and had he taken the trouble to arrive at ten a.m. along with everyone else that morning, his opinion would have been gratefully received and adhered to. However, as he chose not to be there, he had missed the boat, as I was not about to do them all over again. He left even more displeased than when he arrived.

The following morning, still disappointed by Mick's reaction the previous evening, and knowing that he was unhappy with the whole idea of me mixing the record, I rang Joe to say although I had enjoyed working with him immensely, I did not think too much of his mate and thought it best not to continue.

A couple of hours later, I got a call from Muff to say that Mick Jones had apologized and would not participate in the sessions from there on, leaving Joe to be the band's representative at the sessions.

So Joe and I reconvened and had a blast, rerecording a couple of his vocals and mixing the rest of the record in a couple more days. I cannot tell you how much I enjoyed his company. Certainly one of the most genuine people I have ever met. Bright as a button and seemed to me to be totally unaffected by his success. A truly lovely and extremely talented man. A huge loss to the music community when he died in December 2002.

I forgot to mention, the album was *Combat Rock*. There were two hit singles from it: "Rock the Casbah" and the even more popular "Should I Stay or Should I Go."

It must have been extremely difficult for Mick to let go of the record that he had invested so much time and effort in. It would be hard to just give it to some complete stranger to mess with. He was good enough to let me get on with it, and when the dust settled, he seemed happy enough with the result, as I was to find out at our next meeting, where he was extremely pleasant.

A few months later I was making a live album with The Who on tour in America. The Clash opened for them on a few gigs, and they asked, as I was there with the gear, could I record them as well. I was happy to oblige, and did so at Shea Stadium in New York and the Coliseum in Los Angeles. All I remember is a lot of manic energy, not a good sound, and the bass player seemed to be on some other nonmusical planet. Nothing usable, in my opinion, but I understand that some of those recordings have since been released to feed the insatiable appetite of Clash fans by their record company.

I was fortunate to remain pals with Joe, and he returned to my studio to produce an album with his longtime friend from art school Tymon Dogg. That, sadly, was the last time I saw him.

PARICIPANTS IN THE ARMS CONCERT TOUR OF AMERICA. IN VARIOUS
GROUPINGS: RONNIE LANE, ERIC CLAPTON, JIMMY PAGE, JEFF BECK,
BILL WYMAN, CHARLIE WATTS, JOE COCKER, PAUL RODGERS, KENNY
JONES, ANDY FAIRWEATHER LOW, RAY COOPER, JAMES NEWTON,
CHRIS STAINTON, SIMON PHILIPS, JAN HAMMER, FERNANDO
SAUNDERS, BILL GRAHAM, AND ME.

ARMS, 1983

As a result of his hit single "How Come?" in 1973, Ronnie Lane got a deal with A&M records and used the money from the advance to buy a derelict farm in Wales. He moved there with his wife and kids to become a sheep farmer while still writing songs and recording them with the mobile unit he had built in an Airstream caravan while he was in the Faces. That is, when it was available. It was in constant demand from the likes of Bad Company and Led Zeppelin. The income that this produced helped to keep his head above water while making the farmhouse livable. Ronnie recorded a couple of albums there. He was so broke that he used the same few reels of two-inch tape over and over again. Erasing the previous album in order to make the next.

Stu and Eric Clapton would often go down to play with Ronnie, both enjoying the solitude of the farm and hanging out with their friend playing music. Stu came round to see me after one of these visits and told me that he was becoming increasingly concerned about Ronnie, as he was slurring his words and losing his balance as if he were drunk. At first, no one paid much attention, thinking he probably was. Until one day, when he complained that his arm had pins and needles and had become numb, making it difficult for him to play.

Pretty soon he had been diagnosed with multiple sclerosis, but only as a result of Stu and his wife, Cynthia, insisting that he go and get checked out, as up to then Ronnie had been in complete denial. Ronnie stayed with them when he went to London, and it was dear Cynthia who recommended a form of treatment that temporarily eased the symptoms of the disease using a hyperbaric oxygen chamber. They are tanks commonly used to decompress deep-sea divers. As there was only one available for use in London, Ronnie decided to try and raise £20,000 to buy another for a charity, Action Research into Multiple Sclerosis, or ARMS, to use exclusively.

He asked Eric if he would do a gig to raise the money. Eric was happy to help and turned to me to help him put a band together. His band was all Americans, so it would have been completely uneconomical to bring them over from the States and put them up in a hotel for one charity concert. I got straight on the phone to Stu, Bill Wyman, Charlie Watts, and Andy Fairweather Low. By the end of the day, all had agreed to do the show for Ronnie.

A few days later, Stu went to a party at Jeff Beck's house. He mentioned to Jeff and Jimmy Page that we were doing the concert and they both offered their services there and then. So the whole thing instantly took on another life. Jimmy had not played since the breakup of Led Zeppelin, and now we had three of the greatest guitar players in Britain appearing on the same bill. The word got out, and pretty soon my phone was ringing off the hook with equipment companies' road managers and the rock and roll elite offering their services in droves, responding to the request for help from one of their own. Their generosity was completely out of kilter with the media's image of them as preening, self-important, spoiled brats.

As Eric had previously been discussing the possibility of doing a concert for Prince Charles's Trust, he suggested that the promoter, Harvey Goldsmith, book two nights at the Albert Hall and kill two birds with one stone.

Being completely out of my depth, I approached Paddy Grafton Green, the kindest man on the planet and the best lawyer in London, for help with the legal aspect of things. He readily donated an enormous amount of his time to the charity. I sold the radio rights in America to raise the cash to pay for our concert to be filmed, then rang Stanley Dorfman in L.A., who dropped everything and flew to London at his own expense to come and direct it. He was the only man for the job as he already had a wonderful relationship with everyone on the bill, having worked with them all many times in his days directing *Top of the Pops* and *In Concert* for the BBC. There is no one to touch him when it comes to shooting live music. His knowledge, respect, and enthusiasm for music and musicians is as deep and wide as anyone I know, bringing a wonderful aura of calm with all that expertise and sympathy to his work.

Eric invited his old pal Stevie Winwood and added Ray Cooper on percussion to his band. Kenney Jones could not be left out, as he had been in the Faces and the Small Faces with Ronnie.

We rehearsed at my place for a week. They all came from far and wide. No one was ever late. There was never a glimmer of ego from anyone. Although Jeff was rehearsing his own band elsewhere, he still came to our rehearsals every day, so as to be there should we need him. The whole spirit of the event revolved around Ronnie and everyone's affection for him. No one minded where they were on the bill. I think it was the first concert of its type where everyone played with one another. My idea being to give the audience an experience they had not seen before and were not likely to see again.

Ronnie's cheerful presence never let us lose sight of why we were there, and by the end of the week I think we were all pleasantly surprised, as it was something very few of us had experienced. It was hysterically funny, very social, and fantastic to be involved with, as everyone got on so well.

The first of the two nights was for Prince Charles's Trust. We were all lined up to meet him and Princess Diana before the show. Poor Princess Diana, she was only twenty-two, so had not got a clue who she was meeting, as we all came from another era of music than she was likely to have been interested in. I tried to explain who was who and she responded in a shy and grateful way as if she understood but I am sure that she didn't.

As it was Eric that had been approached to do this show, it did not have quite the same importance to the rest of us, and although we were happy to do it for a very good cause, I think some of us treated it like a good run-through for the following night for Ronnie. Andy Zweck from Harvey's office took over responsibility for the production office at the venue, so everything ran like clockwork. The concerts were a wonderful success for all who took part. The end being particularly emotional with Ronnie coming onstage with everyone and singing "Goodnight Irene." There was not a dry eye in the house. Along with me, I am sure that any individual in the audience felt extremely fortunate to be there.

The Stones donated their truck for me to record the radio show and sound for the video that we sold to Laurence Ronson, father to the record producer Mark and younger brother of the British business tycoon and philanthropist Gerald Ronson. Through his exceptional generosity and the fact that it was completely sold out, we ended up raising more than $1 million from the night.

We all met backstage after the show and, having had such a blast putting the whole thing together, decided that all that hard work should not go to waste, so we should consider doing more shows, and arranged to have dinner at my house a few days later to discuss the possibility of where and when.

It was clear that this combination of the principal musicians who took part with Eric at the helm had a far greater earning power than any of them as individuals.

They all attended the dinner, where after much discussion, it was decided that we should take it to America. Stu suggested that Bill Graham was the only promoter in the States to handle the job and who they all knew and trusted. Having been charged with calling him, Stu returned to the table five minutes later to inform us that Bill was with us and the services of his entire company were at our disposal.

A month later I was dispatched to San Francisco to meet with Bill and sort out the details of the tour. My only previous knowledge of him was negative gossip and the one decidedly unpleasant meeting all those years ago with Steve Miller. In short, I did not trust him, so I felt like a Christian being fed to the lions as I boarded that plane, as you could write everything I knew about touring on a postage stamp.

On arrival I nervously explained that my principal concern was to maximize the amount of money raised by not wasting it on the frivolous expenditure that is so often associated with fund-raising. My fears were soon put to rest. Bill was nowhere near as intimidating as I expected. He could so easily have taken advantage of my complete ignorance of concert promotion but instead patiently steered me through the process of setting up the tour and maximizing the profit from it. Mick Brigden from Bill's office took over the day-to-day logistics and tour management, holding my hand through the many pitfalls we experienced.

While in San Francisco I received a call from Eric's manager to say that Steve Winwood had dropped out and that I had twenty-four hours to find a replacement or the whole thing was off. I called Joe Cocker and thank God he was available, as we could not have found a better replacement. Eric was okay with the idea, so after a few hours of flat panic we were back on again with three weeks to go until the first date in Dallas. We played nine shows in America and broke box office records in most of them, ending up with a fantastic reception at Madison Square Garden, the tour raising a total of around $1 million.

The following day on the plane back to London, it suddenly came to me that I had tricked myself into believing that all that effort and outpouring of affection for Ronnie from so many people over the previous few weeks would, like some kind of fairy story, somehow cure him of this terrible debilitating disease. This was not to be.

It seemed to me that, as we were raising money from Americans, it was only fair to use it to establish ARMS in America and encourage collaboration and exchange of the research that already existed in Great Britain. So a few months later, the charity was established in America via a lawyer who said she was in remission from MS and who offered her services to Ronnie to run it from her offices in Houston. In an effort to gain more publicity for the cause, we were all taken to Houston and given the freedom of the city, along with a warm message of endorsement from President Reagan. His kind acknowledgment of what we had achieved proved invaluable when,

several months later, it was discovered that the lawyer had misappro-
priated a substantial amount of the money we had raised. Ronnie
wrote to President Reagan for help and he was absolved of any responsibility but it must have had a hugely adverse effect on a man
who was seriously ill to begin with.

He went to live in Austin, Texas, making many friends, becoming
a well-loved fringe member of the music community. Sitting in at
the odd gig around town with people like Joe Ely, when his health
allowed.

He married his nurse, Susan, and eventually moved to Colorado,
where he died in June 1997, living out his last days unable to move
but never losing his wicked sense of humor. His courage and honesty
touched everyone he came in contact with, and as Joe Ely says, "He
is still with us through the songs he wrote."

THE ARTISTS FOR THE ALBERT HALL GIG FOR ARMS. FROM LEFT,
BACK ROW: JIMMY PAGE, CHARLIE WATTS, CHRIS STAINTON, JEFF
BECK, STEVIE WINWOOD, RAY COOPER, FERNANDO SAUNDERS,
ANDY FAIRWEATHER LOW, AND BILL WYMAN. FRONT ROW:
KENNEY JONES, RONNIE LANE, ERIC CLAPTON, AND ME.

The Eighties
and Nineties

Over the next few years I made more albums with Joan Armatrading, Andy Fairweather Low, The Who, and Eric Clapton. The results of my efforts to work with new artists like Live Wire for A&M, Charlie Dore for Chrysalis, and the wonderful guitar player Tim Renwick for CBS falling on stony ground. I was finding it more and more difficult to find new artists I wanted to work with, and in equal part, what I was doing began to sound dated and perhaps a little tired.

In 1979, Jerry Moss approached me with the idea of us going into partnership to build a studio in London, and A&M bought the huge old Regal Cinema in Fulham for the purpose. A&M was the company with the most artist-friendly feel of any of the labels that I dealt with. This was because it was owned and run by Jerry and Herb Alpert who set the tone and, with very few exceptions, employed people who maintained it. While remaining a serious business enterprise under Jerry's watchful eye and I am sure with Abe Somer's good counsel, they managed to preserve the image of the company's insatiable appetite and enthusiasm for good music. Not an easy task.

I look back with great affection on those warm sunny California afternoons spent hanging out on the balcony of David's office, watching the pretty secretaries going about their business—tripping backward and forwards across the lot—while discussing the pros and cons of what was happening in the business.

Jerry changed his mind and decided not to go ahead with the studio in London and sold the building. So, having spent some considerable time meeting with architects, acquiring equipment, and starting to build a console, I decided to continue with the project on my own and build a residential studio out in the English countryside. Twelve months later, I had bought a small farm in West Sussex, and with a great deal of help from Stu, converted its stable block into a studio.

I fell in love with the house, and although it had not been my original intention, moved into it, spending the next twenty-five years living there while working with The Who, The Clash, Bob Dylan, Midnight Oil, Jools Holland, New Model Army, the French band Téléphone, Emmylou Harris and Linda Ronstadt, David Crosby, Labi Siffre, and Helen Watson, among many others. Every now and then I would go back to work in America, where, to be honest, I felt much more comfortable musically. I became more and more disenchanted with what was happening in the UK, and it increasingly became more disenchanted with me. The synthesizer and the drum machine took over and, to my mind, the standard of songwriting plummeted, with people becoming obsessed with beats per minute and electronically created sounds that in the end all sounded the same to me.

I continued to seek out and work with the ever-diminishing number of great songwriters and singers who still had a record deal and a fan base. John Hiatt was at the forefront. He is an exceptional talent and certainly is up there with the best songwriters I have worked with. His lyrics are superb, having the extraordinary ability to paint a picture or describe an emotion in one line that would take any mere mortal an entire page.

I was turned on to him by Andy Fairweather Low, who rang me one day bursting with excitement, as he had been following Ry Cooder round the country on his tour of Great Britain, saying that Ry had one of the best singers he had ever heard performing with him.

John was on A&M, and when I was asked to work with him, he had already made the superb album *Bring the Family* for them. This is probably the best album he has ever made, and being the well-oiled machine they had become, John, Ry Cooder, Jim Keltner and Nick Lowe only took four days to make it.

It was recorded by the exceptionally talented engineer Larry Hirsch. Being so impressed with the sound, I asked him to engineer for me when I produced John's album *Slow Turning*. This was the first time I relinquished the role of engineer on any record I made. At first I felt like a spare part, not quite knowing where to put myself, but I soon got used to it and found it really refreshing not to have to do two jobs at once.

We recorded in Nashville at Ronnie Milsap's Groundstar Labs, using John's road band as the rhythm section that included the amazing Sonny Landreth on slide guitar and Kenneth Blevins on drums, adding Bernie Leadon playing guitars various and the wonderful James Hooker on keyboards. I took it to L.A. to mix at Ocean Way. Thanks to the owner, Allen Sides, this was one of the few remaining studios that had stayed true to the acoustics for which they were originally designed in the late fifties, not succumbing to the commercial pressure of having SSL consoles and Hidley acoustic designs, both of which have been responsible for systematically reducing the quality of recorded sound like some invidious cancer.

Having finished *Slow Turning*, John's manager, Ken Levitan, invited me back to Nashville to meet with Nanci Griffith with the view of me producing her next album. He took us both out to dinner, after which I was not convinced that I should work with her, as we seemed to have little in common as personalities. The following morning James Hooker rang to tell me I was making a big mistake and that Nanci was extremely shy but once you got to know her she became a great deal less reserved. So I took him at his word and agreed to make the album on the understanding that it was my intention to take her out of the glass case that she resided in and put her in a cardboard box. Nanci seemed quite happy with this and bravely went along with pretty much whatever I ran by her, whether she completely understood or not, and rose to the occasion with flying colors. She was perfectly polite and professional, but as I had originally suspected, she never really seemed to loosen up. We came from different planets as far as our personalities were concerned. I don't think this affected the record at all, just the experience of making it.

I used Fran Breen, drums; Pat Donaldson, bass; Neill MacColl and Bernie Leadon, guitars; and the brothers, Jerry and Mark Donahue, electric guitar and emulator, respectively; with James Hooker, keyboards, and moral support for Nanci. They all made a significant contribution and along with Jack Joseph Puig's engineering, complemented Nanci's songs and her impeccable performance of them.

The second album I made for John Hiatt, *Stolen Moments*, was recorded in 1990 at Ocean Way, and this time, in an effort to make the record sound more contemporary, I decided to use Jack

Puig to engineer. He had developed his own way of working and turned up with a truckload of his own equipment, which completely filled the control room and involved a rat's nest of cables, to integrate it with the perfectly adequate equipment that was already there, much to my annoyance.

We had first met in 1987 when he visited me on a session for the album *Blue Slipper* by the superb English singer-songwriter Helen Watson at A&M studios in Los Angeles. I had put a fantastic band together with Richie Hayward, drums; Bill Payne, piano; and Paul Barrere, guitar—all from Little Feat. George Hawkins, bass; Paul "Wix" Wickens, keyboards; Michael Landau, Steve Lukather, Bernie Leadon, and Jerry Donahue on guitars. The word had got out that I was making an album with a large rhythm section playing live in the studio, and as this had already become something of a novelty, it created some interest from some of the younger engineers in town, who were anxious to see how it was done and to check out this incredible combination of musicians. Jack came by and politely introduced himself, asking if he could sit in and watch for a while. I was immediately struck by his intensity and enthusiasm for engineering, being as a large piece of blotting paper, anxious to absorb as much information as he could, while remaining extremely respectful and not interfering with the proceedings.

Prior to starting *Stolen Moments*, John and I met up in his hometown of Nashville in order for us to discuss the material and the musicians we felt would be suitable for the record. John asked if I would accompany him to check out a rhythm section he knew of in Memphis, with the view of using them on the album. To pass the time during the long drive from Nashville, I played him a cassette of some demos that my son Ethan had just sent me from England. I had let him loose in my studio at home whenever I was not using it, and he took full advantage, writing, playing, and recording his own material, becoming more and more accomplished as a musician, engineer, and songwriter. John was really impressed with Ethan's playing, and when the guys in Memphis turned out not to be suitable, he suggested that we use him on drums for the album. I completely disagreed with the idea, not wanting to be accused of nepotism, but John insisted, saying it was not open for discussion. I don't know who was more nervous on the first session, Ethan or me. The first song we cut was "Child of the Wild Blue Yonder" and John threw Ethan right in at the deep end by suggesting that the song should start with four bars of drums. I cannot tell you how relieved and proud I was when he pulled it off. Not trying to impress or show off but playing just what was required. He went on to play a blistering solo on electric guitar that put the icing on the cake. After that John and I used him wherever possible on the rest of the album, playing acoustic and electric guitar, mandolin, and percussion. Having the experience of playing with and being encouraged by John and the elite musicians Richie Hayward, Pat Donaldson, Mike Landau, Wix, and Chuck Leavell was the making of him, and started a relationship between us that very few parents are fortunate enough to experience—working together in a creative environment on several albums over the next few years.

Just like Eric Clapton and me, John was a huge fan of JJ Cale. In conversation one day I mentioned that I had always wanted to work with Mac Gayden, the amazing slide guitar player on Cale's album *Naturally*. We were close to finishing the record and John suggested that we find him and bring him to L.A. to overdub him on the last two tracks that needed work. John told me that Mr. Gayden had had an unfortunate experience with LSD from which he had never quite recovered and had become something of a recluse. In any event, he was tracked down and he agreed to come and play, much to my excitement.

On his arrival at the studio, it quickly became apparent that while remaining polite and softly spoken, Mac was living in his own mental space, which made communication tricky. Additionally, he struggled to comprehend the arrangement or contribute anything that made much sense for either of the two songs we wanted him to play on.

I had the most enormous respect for this man and it was terribly sad to witness what he had become. John was so embarrassed that he left me to it. So, determined to give Mac every opportunity, I gave him a cassette of the two songs and made him comfortable in the lounge with a sound system, telling him to take all the time he needed to familiarize himself with the songs, while I returned to the control room and started to mix the rest of the album.

Woody Allen once said, "Leave the artist alone and you will get a performance from them that came from the reason you booked them." It is a principle I have always tried to adhere to. The reason for booking any musician is to facilitate their natural skills with respect and hope that their chemistry works with others. There is little point in getting a dog and barking yourself.

After a couple of hours I asked Mac if he would like to make another attempt at "Thirty Years of Tears." He agreed and we set him up in the studio and played him the song. After running it through a few times nothing much had changed and he still did not have anything close to a grasp of it. So I brought him into the control room, thinking that might make him feel more comfortable and so that I could talk to him face-to-face rather than through the somewhat impersonal use of earphones. After several more attempts, the situation remained the same and it looked like we were going to have to abandon the session.

Now, I love this song. The lyric relates to a tragic event in the past that is never emotionally dealt with and as a result subconsciously creates a barrier of anger that prevents any possibility of true happiness until confronted and dealt with. Something I identify with from my own past.

In one last attempt I said to Mac, "Look, I just want you to make me cry." I ran the tape and he proceeded to play the most amazing, heart-wrenching guitar part. Climaxing with a solo that still brings a tear to my eye whenever I hear it. With one simple sentence I had finally found a way to get through to him in his altered state, and he proved what I had believed all along, that there was still an amazing musician in there fighting to get out.

I am really proud of the two albums I made with John. It was a treat and a privilege to work with him and I learned a great deal from the experience.

At Ken Levitan's suggestion, we got together one more time in 2001 to record the songs John wrote for the Disney movie *The Country Bears*. John's material, performance, and input were exemplary, and although the script looked great, the film was a disaster of massive incompetence in every other respect. The only positives to come out of it were working with John again and the music supervisor Nora Felder and her pal from Disney's music production office, Monica Zierhut, who were anything but incompetent and made the job almost bearable. However, the whole experience convinced me that the movie business and I were definitely not suited.

Then there came an album with Crosby, Stills & Nash in L.A., with Ethan playing drums and guitars. This came about because we had cut a couple of tracks with Crosby for a solo album at my studio in England and he insisted that Ethan play on the album with CSN. This resulted in Ethan going on the road with them for the next year, with Graham Nash keeping a fatherly eye on him for me. For which I shall be eternally grateful.

I saw out the tail end of the twentieth century by making albums with Tanya Donelly's band Belly, at Chris Blackwell's Compass Point Studios in Nassau; the extraordinary guitar player Joe Satriani; and a solo album with Linda Ronstadt at the fabulous residential studio the Site in Northern California. Then I produced a duet album with Linda and Emmylou Harris at a house in the grounds of a hotel in Tucson, Arizona, and produced and mixed tracks of duets with Emmylou Harris and Sheryl Crow in L.A., Evan Dando and Juliana Hatfield in Boston, Lucinda Williams and David Crosby in Nashville, and a solo performance with Elvis Costello for an album in tribute to Gram Parsons for Jerry Moss's new label, Almo Sounds. A diverse and stimulating mix of talent.

Still feeling that my sound was dated, I relied on Jack Puig and my incredibly overqualified assistant from Ocean Way, Steve "Idle Toad" Holroyd, to engineer these sessions, in an attempt to try and keep me contemporary, calling on my son Ethan, Andy Fairweather Low, Bernie Leadon, Mike Campbell, Benmont Tench, Carlos Vega, Nathan East, Manu Katché, Greg Leisz, Wix, the McGarrigle sisters, Neil Young, and Helen Watson, among others, to contribute their collective skills in the process.

I was a little intimidated by the fact that my brother Andy had already made a fantastic-sounding album with Joe and the Bissonette brothers. I put together the finest guys that I could find in order to both keep up with and challenge Joe for the self-titled *Joe Satriani* album. They sure did the job and Joe rose to the occasion brilliantly, playing live with the rhythm section for the majority of the record. Not something he was used to doing.

I was invited to produce this record by Joe's manager, Mick Brigden. Having become good friends while working on the ARMS tour in America, we had kept in touch. By this time, Bill Graham had been killed in a helicopter accident and his business eventually sold, leaving Mick to manage Joe and go on to establish a vineyard in Sonoma Valley along with his gorgeous wife Julia, or "Girl" as she is affectionately known. Some twenty-five years previously I had produced "Quicksilver Girl," a song that had been written by Steve Miller about her, as she had once been married to David Freiberg, the bass player and singer with the band Quicksilver Messenger Service.

It was while staying at Mick and Julia's that the idea for this book was first put to me over lunch. It was their enthusiasm, along with much encouragement and bullying from my friend Keryn Kaplan in New York, that gave me the courage to even attempt it.

WITH CROSBY, STILLS & NASH. ALL FOUR OF US TRYING TO EXPRESS OUR OPINIONS MORE CONVINCINGLY THAN ANYONE ELSE. FROM LEFT: STEPHEN STILLS, DAVID CROSBY, GRAHAM NASH AND ME.

Fred Walecki

In the summer of 2000, Bernie Leadon called me in England with the terrible news that our mutual friend Fred Walecki had been diagnosed with throat cancer. Bernie had introduced me to Fred in the early seventies as *the* guy for acoustic guitars. He owned a store on Westwood Boulevard in Los Angeles that was frequented by everyone who was anyone in the music community. The first time we met, I bought three fantastic guitars and made a friend for life. I was bowled over by this genial, gentle man with an extraordinary vocabulary that was very rarely allowed to rest. He could talk the hind leg off a donkey. This making it all the worse when we were informed that as part of his treatment he was to have his voice box removed. I was aware that business had not been so good for the store for a while and suspected that one of the first cutbacks that Freddie may have had to make was his health insurance. Bernie and

I decided to put on a concert to raise the substantial amount of money his treatment would cost. This proved really simple to do as he was known and loved by so many artists and musicians who he had gone out of his way to help over the years.

Pretty soon we had a star-studded cast of thousands: Warren Zevon, Jackson Browne, Crosby and Nash, Bonnie Raitt, Colin Hay from Men at Work, the amazing actor Jeff Bridges (who went to school with Fred), Chris Hillman and Herb Pedersen, Emmylou Harris, Linda Ronstadt, Randy Meisner, Spiñal Tap, and Don Henley. The solo artists were supported by a house band consisting of Ry Cooder, Jennifer Condos, Ethan Johns, Albert Lee, Andy Fairweather Low, Paul "Wix" Wickens, and Bernie. There are few individuals who could summon such a response from so many to a call for help, and it is a fair testament to the man, who may be the only true Christian soul I have ever come across.

We rehearsed for a few days, everyone working tirelessly to make the show the remarkable success it became. As with the ARMS concert, there was never a glimmer of ego from anyone involved. I have one outstanding memory of the rehearsals: Ry Cooder turning up driving a flatbed truck with his guitar and amp in the back, and him quietly, without fuss, unloading and setting up his own gear in the room. This may not seem like much, but normally artists of his stature have a team that arrive ahead of time to set everything up so that they can arrive and pick up their already tuned instrument and start playing. He played guitar for Jackson Browne and was the highlight of the entire concert for me.

We sold out the Santa Monica Civic Auditorium for two nights. The audience certainly got great value for their money. Particularly on the first night, when Roger McGuinn turned up, resulting in The

Byrds getting together for the first time since 1990 and singing "Turn! Turn! Turn!" and "Mr. Tambourine Man," which caused the audience to take the roof off the place.

Freddie bravely took the stage at the end of each night to thank the artists and audience alike, using a device that is held to the throat and quietly emits a monotone machine-like voice. You could have heard a pin drop in the auditorium. The silence only being broken by the great bursts of laughter in reaction to his hysterically funny speech, with him effortlessly managing to use humor to deflect any thought of sympathy for his newfound condition.

FRED THANKING THE ENSEMBLE FOR THEIR EFFORTS AT THE END OF THE SHOW AT SANTA MONICA CIVIC AUDITORIUM.

Ashes and Fire

The entire music business seemed to slowly drift further and further away from me over the next few years. While never considering myself retired, I happily came to terms with my new life of leisure. Always believing that it was not quite over yet.

In early 2011, I received a surprise call from Ryan Adams, asking me if I would be at all interested in making an album with him. Ryan had made three of my favorite albums: *Pneumonia*, with his band Whiskeytown, in 1999; *Heartbreaker* in 2000; and finally *Gold* in 2001. All produced by my son. Unfortunately, Ryan's alcohol and substance abuse at the time brought their working relationship to a premature end. I was a huge fan of these records and over the next few years I did all I could to encourage Ethan to patch it up and work with him again, as they were a formidable team. I visited many of their sessions and became a huge fan of Ryan, believing him to be head and shoulders above his songwriting contemporaries.

So here we are ten years later. A reformed character on the phone. Clean, straight, married to the gorgeous Mandy Moore, and ready to make a new album. He had already spoken to Ethan, who was booked for some months, and so at Ethan's suggestion had decided to give me a call. I jumped at the opportunity and we went ahead and made *Ashes & Fire* at Sunset Sound in Los Angeles. The first musician I booked was Jeremy Stacey, the genius drummer who was recommended to me by Ethan. In turn, Jeremy recommended two bass players, neither of whom I knew. Gus Seyffert, who played brilliantly, and Sam Dixon, who only got to play on one song but really did himself proud. Ryan asked his friend Norah Jones to play piano, and I asked Benmont Tench to come and play Hammond organ and electric piano. Everyone was excited about the idea of working with Ryan and with one another. The perfect environment in which to make a record.

It was a blast. All of the musicians stepping up to the plate and delivering superb support for Ryan, with Norah and Benmont adding wonderful textures while still managing to respectfully stay out of each other's way. For his part, Ryan delivered breathtaking live performances. All of which were achieved in only one or two takes.

With encouragement from others, I decided that my sound was no longer dated and after a gap of many years reverted back to recording what I produced. Much to my relief, I fell straight back into it, just like riding a bike.

We finished up the sessions by adding the Section, a string quartet consisting of Daphne Chen, Lauren Chipman, and Richard Dodd, and led by Eric Gorfain. Ryan had worked with them before and

WITH RYAN
ADAMS AND
NORAH JONES
AT THE *ASHES &
FIRE* SESSIONS
AT SUNSET
SOUND, LOS
ANGELES.

ME, EXPRESSING MY OPINION LOUDER THAN ANYONE ELSE
TO THE WONDERFUL BEN BRIDWELL OF BAND OF HORSES
AT SUNSET SOUND IN L.A.

strongly recommended them. I had never done a string session without the arrangement having been written beforehand, but Ryan assured me this was not necessary as they were quite accustomed to doing one on the spot. They proved to be every bit as good as he said, writing and performing beautiful string parts on four of the songs.

The release of this album came a few months later, Ryan's huge fan base putting it in the Top 10 in England and America. I was back in the saddle and really enjoying myself.

Next came an album with Ben Bridwell's Band of Horses. A nicer bunch of guys you could not wish to meet. We worked hard and made an album that we were all proud of. Ben and I made a really good connection. I really admire his conviction and work ethic and hope that one day we will get the opportunity to work together again.

Surprisingly, for the first time in my memory, there are two guys running record companies that are musicians. Dan McCarroll and Don Was. A more genuine and talented rhythm section you will not find. Whether they will survive the battering their integrity will receive in the dog-eat-dog world they have landed in, we will have to wait and see. I really wish them well. I would not be in their shoes for all the tea in China.

Dan was responsible for releasing Ryan's record *Ashes & Fire* on Capitol, and I recently had the pleasure of mixing the Aaron Neville album *My True Story* and a couple of tracks for the Stones' fiftieth-anniversary album for Don. He, in return, came and played bass for me on some Ryan Adams songs and on an album that I produced with my pal Benmont Tench, the genius keyboard player with Tom Petty and the Heartbreakers, that he ended up acquiring for release on Blue Note.

Benmont's album *You Should Be So Lucky* and the experience of making it sum up the best and most positive aspects of what I have been doing for the past fifty years. A group of like-minded individuals getting together to play music with and pay tribute to one of their peers without any thought of financial recompense. If it should turn out to be the last record I make, I shall shuffle off this mortal coil with a large grin on my face.

BENMONT TENCH, ME, AND DON WAS. SESSION FOR *YOU SHOULD BE SO LUCKY* AT SUNSET SOUND.

2014

In the past few years, the music business has gone through the most tumultuous changes. Most of the independent labels have been absorbed by the majors and the majors in turn have merged with each other. It seems to have gone full circle, with the industry having reverted back to just a handful of corporate labels. Just like it was when I started in 1959.

Gone are the days of a new artist being signed and nurtured over a period of two or three years, with the record company providing tour support in order to promote record sales. Today, this has turned 180 degrees, with the label taking a percentage of the artist's earnings on the road, as in most cases record sales alone can no longer justify the investment they have to make.

Recorded music has been reduced to ones and zeros. The quality of reproduction and delivery has become less and less important to the listener. I wonder where it will all lead to. The business as I know it is seriously under threat, barely surviving on its past glories. Things cannot stand still. Maybe there will be another huge shake-up, with the teenagers of today taking the industry by the scruff of the neck and reinventing it. The next few years will be fascinating to watch. Of course, popular music will survive and it will throw up many more fascinating characters, but it is becoming increasingly difficult to sustain as a business in its present form. I think I may well have had the best of it.

This all began with me being introduced as an eight-year-old into my local church choir and it having the most positive effect through the physical and emotional pleasure it brought me. Several quirks of fate somehow led to a career in the record business, meeting along the way some of the extraordinary individuals who have played a major role in the development of popular music to the present day.

If you ever feel a bit low or feel that life has become a little mundane, join a choir. I guarantee that it will lift your spirits. Who knows what it will lead to. Look what happened to me.

ACKNOWLEDGMENTS

My heartfelt thanks to the following for their encouragement, guidance, and support: Sarah Hochman, David Rosenthal, Keryn Kaplan, Bill Flanagan, Glynis Johns, Charley, Abigail and Ethan Johns, and Will Nash.

And for taking the time and trouble to provide me with photographs or information that I could not recall: Ethan Russell, Gered Mankovitz, Will Nash, Bill Wyman, Henry Diltz, Bernie Leadon, Andrew Oldham, Chris Kimsey, Angela Close, Ryan Adams, Derek Green, Steve Holroyd, Russ Shagbaum.

And a special thanks to Robert Greenfield and Fred Schruers for their time and invaluable input.

SELECT DISCOGRAPHY
(ALBUMS ONLY)
Compiled by Andrew Alburn

1964

Georgie Fame, *Rhythm and Blues at the Flamingo*; engineer, mixing

1965

The Rolling Stones, *December's Children (And Everybody's)*; engineer, mixing

The Pretty Things, *Get the Picture?*; producer, engineer, mixing

The Rolling Stones, *Out of Our Heads*; engineer, mixing

1966

The Rolling Stones, *Aftermath*; engineer, mixing

The Rolling Stones, *Got Live If You Want It!*; engineer, mixing

Chris Farlowe, *The Art of Chris Farlowe*; engineer, mixing

Small Faces, *Small Faces* (Decca); engineer, mixing

Chris Farlowe, *14 Things to Think About*; engineer, mixing

Twice as Much, *Own Up*; engineer, mixing

1967
Small Faces, *From the Beginning*; engineer, mixing

Small Faces, *Small Faces* (Immediate); engineer, mixing

The Rolling Stones, *Their Satanic Majesties Request*; engineer, mixing

The Rolling Stones, *Between the Buttons*; engineer, mixing

The Rolling Stones, *Flowers*; engineer, mixing

Johnny Hallyday, *San Francisco* EP; engineer

1968
The Rolling Stones, *Beggars Banquet*; engineer, mixing

Steve Miller Band, *Children of the Future*; producer, engineer, mixing

Twice as Much, *That's All*; engineer

The Pentangle, *The Pentangle*; engineer, mixing

The Move, *Something Else from the Move*; engineer, mixing

Spooky Tooth, *It's All About*; engineer, mixing

Small Faces, *Ogdens' Nut Gone Flake*; engineer, mixing

Steve Miller Band, *Sailor*; producer, engineer, mixing

Gerry Temple, *Burn Up!*; engineer

Procol Harum, *Shine On Brightly*; engineer, mixing

The Move, *The Move*; engineer, mixing

The Easybeats, *Vigil*; engineer, mixing

Traffic, *Traffic*; engineer, mixing

Billy Nicholls, *Would You Believe*; engineer, mixing

1969

Steve Miller Band, *Brave New World*; producer, engineer, mixing

Family, *Family Entertainment*; producer, engineer, mixing

The End, *Introspection*; engineer, mixing

The Beatles, *Abbey Road*; engineer

Joe Cocker, *Joe Cocker!*; engineer, mixing

Johnny Hallyday, *Johnny Hallyday*; producer, engineer, mixing

Led Zeppelin, *Led Zeppelin*; director of engineering, engineer

The Rolling Stones, *Let It Bleed*; engineer, mixing

Steve Miller Band, *Your Saving Grace*; producer, engineer, mixing

1970

Lambert and Nuttycombe, *At Home*; engineer, producer

The Rolling Stones, *Get Yer Ya-Ya's Out!*; producer, engineer, mixing

Humble Pie, *Humble Pie*; producer, engineer, mixing

Philamore Lincoln, *The North Wind Blew South*; engineer

Billy Preston, *That's the Way God Planned It*; engineer, mixing

Leon Russell, *Leon Russell*; engineer, mixing

The Beatles, *Let It Be*; engineer

Joe Cocker, *Mad Dogs & Englishmen*; producer, mixing

Delaney & Bonnie & Friends, *On Tour with Eric Clapton*; engineer

The Move, *Shazam*; engineer, mixing

The Band, *Stage Fright*; mixing

Spooky Tooth, *The Last Puff*; engineer, mixing

McGuinness Flint, *McGuinness Flint*; producer, engineer, mixing

1971

Faces, *A Nod Is as Good as a Wink . . . to a Blind Horse*; producer, engineer, mixing

Boz Scaggs, *Boz Scaggs & Band*; producer, engineer, mixing

Ben Sidran, *Feel Your Groove*; engineer, liner notes, mixing

McGuinness Flint, *Happy Birthday, Ruthy Baby*; producer, engineer, mixing

Jesse Ed Davis, *Jesse Davis*; producer, engineer, mixing

Leon Russell, *Leon Russell and the Shelter People*; engineer, mixing

Boz Scaggs, *Moments*; producer, engineer, mixing

Rita Coolidge, *Nice Feelin'*; engineer

Humble Pie, *Rock On*; producer, engineer, mixing

Graham Nash, *Songs for Beginners*; mixing

The Rolling Stones, *Sticky Fingers*; engineer, mixing engineer, mixing

Spooky Tooth, *Tobacco Road*; engineer, mixing

The Who, *Who's Next*; producer, engineer, mixing

1972

Eagles, *Eagles*; producer, engineer, mixing

The Rolling Stones, *Exile on Main St.*; engineer, mixing

Rita Coolidge, *The Lady's Not for Sale*; producer, engineer, mixing

Neil Young, *Harvest*; engineer

Nicky Hopkins, Ry Cooder, Mick Jagger, Bill Wyman, Charlie Watts, *Jamming with Edward!*; producer, engineer, mixing

1973

Chris Jagger, *Chris Jagger*; mixing

Eagles, *Desperado*; producer, engineer, mixing

Eric Clapton, *Eric Clapton's Rainbow Concert*; engineer

Faces, *Ooh La La*; producer, engineer, mixing

The Who, *Quadrophenia*; associate producer, engineer

Rick Grech, *The Last Five Years*; producer, engineer, mixing

Paul McCartney and Wings, *Red Rose Speedway*; engineer

Gallagher & Lyle, *Seeds*; producer, engineer, mixing

The Ozark Mountain Daredevils, *The Ozark Mountain Daredevils*; co-producer, engineer, mixing

Gallagher & Lyle, *Willie and the Lapdog*; producer, engineer, mixing

1974

The Ozark Mountain Daredevils, *It'll Shine When It Shines*; co-producer, engineer, mixing

The Rolling Stones, *It's Only Rock 'n' Roll*; mixing

Eagles, *On the Border*; producer, engineer

Gallagher & Lyle, *The Last Cowboy*; producer, engineer, mixing

Howlin' Wolf, *The London Howlin' Wolf Sessions*; engineer

Georgie Fame, *Georgie Fame*; producer, engineer, mixing

1975

Fairport Convention, *Rising for the Moon*; producer, engineer, mixing

The Who, *The Who by Numbers*; producer, engineer, mixing

1976

Andy Fairweather Low, *Be Bop 'n' Holla*; producer, engineer, mixing

Fools Gold, *Fools Gold*; producer, engineer, mixing

Joan Armatrading, *Joan Armatrading*; producer, engineer, mixing

Ron Wood & Ronnie Lane, *Mahoney's Last Stand*; producer, engineer, mixing

The Rolling Stones, *Black and Blue*; engineer

Buckacre, *Morning Comes*; producer, engineer, mixing

1977

The Bernie Leadon–Michael Georgiades Band, *Natural Progressions*; producer, engineer, mixing

Pete Townshend & Ronnie Lane, *Rough Mix*; producer, engineer, mixing

Joan Armatrading, *Show Some Emotion*; producer, engineer, mixing

Eric Clapton, *Slowhand*; producer, engineer, mixing

1978

Eric Clapton, *Backless*; producer, engineer, mixing

Craig Nuttycombe, *It's Just a Lifetime*; producer, engineer, mixing

Joan Armatrading, *To the Limit*; producer, engineer, mixing

Paul Kennerley and Artists Various, *White Mansions*; producer, engineer, mixing

The Who, *Who Are You*; producer, engineer, mixing

1979

Marc Benno, *Lost in Austin*; producer, engineer, mixing

Joan Armatrading, *Steppin' Out*; producer, engineer, mixing

Live Wire, *Pick It Up*; producer, engineer, mixing

1980

Lazy Racer, *Formula II*; producer, engineer, mixing

Tim Renwick, *Tim Renwick*; producer, engineer, mixing

Paul Kennerley and Artists Various, *Legend of Jesse James*; producer, engineer, mixing

1981

Danny Joe Brown, *Danny Joe Brown and the Danny Joe Brown Band*; producer, engineer, mixing

Jools Holland, *Jools Holland and His Millionaires*; producer, engineer, mixing

Midnight Oil, *Place Without a Postcard*; producer, engineer, mixing

Nine Below Zero, *Don't Point Your Finger*; producer, engineer, mixing

Chris de Burgh, *Best Moves*; producer, engineer, mixing

1982

The Clash, *Combat Rock*; mixing

The Who, *It's Hard*; producer, engineer, mixing

1983

Local Boys, *Moments of Madness*; producer, engineer, mixing

1984

Artists Various, *A.R.M.S. Concert*; producer, engineer, mixing

Jimmy Page, John Paul Jones, Albert Lee, *No Introduction Necessary*; engineer

Téléphone, *Un Autre Monde*; producer, engineer, mixing

1985

Immaculate Fools, *Hearts of Fortune*; mixing

1986

Téléphone, *Le Live*; producer, engineer, mixing

Roaring Boys, *Roaring Boys*; producer, engineer, mixing

The Big Dish, *Swimmer*; producer, engineer, mixing

New Model Army, *The Ghost of Cain*; producer, engineer, mixing

1987

Joolz, *Hex*; mixing

Spooky Tooth, *Spooky Tooth*; engineer, mixing

Helen Watson, *Blue Slipper*; producer, mixing

Labi Siffre, *(Something Inside) So Strong*; producer, engineer, mixing

1988

John Hiatt, *Slow Turning*; producer, mixing

1989

Nanci Griffith, *Storms*; producer, mixing

Green on Red, *This Time Around*; producer, mixing

Helen Watson, *The Weather Inside*; producer, mixing

1990

John Hiatt, *Stolen Moments*; producer, mixing

Summerhill, *West of Here*; mixing

1991

Del Shannon, *The Liberty Years*; engineer

1992

Energy Orchard, *Stop the Machine*; producer, engineer, mixing

Ethan Johns, *Independent Years*; producer, mixing

1993

David Crosby, *Thousand Roads*; producer, engineer, mixing

1994

Crosby, Stills & Nash, *After the Storm*; producer, engineer, mixing

The Subdudes, *Annunciation*; producer, engineer, mixing

Jackopierce, *Bringing on the Weather*; mixing

Bruce Cockburn, *Dart to the Heart*; mixing

1995

Joe Satriani, *Joe Satriani*; producer, mixing

Belly, *King*; producer, mixing

1996

The Beatles, *Anthology 3*; engineer

Eric Clapton, *Crossroads 2: Live in the Seventies*; producer, engineer

Artists Various, *The Rolling Stones Rock and Roll Circus*; engineer, mixing

1997

Warm Jets, *Future Signs*; mixing

1998

Bill Wyman's Rhythm Kings, *Struttin' Our Stuff*; mixing

Linda Ronstadt, *We Ran*; producer, mixing

1999

Bill Wyman's Rhythm Kings, *Anyway the Wind Blows*; mixing

Emmylou Harris & Linda Ronstadt, *Western Wall: The Tucson Sessions*; producer, engineer, mixing

The Pretenders & Emmylou Harris, Elvis Costello, Evan Dando & Juliana Hatfield, Lucinda Williams & David Crosby, *Return of the Grievous Angel*; producer, engineer, mixing

2002

John Hiatt and Artists Various, *Disney's The Country Bears*; musical direction

2005

Bruce Cockburn, *Speechless*; mixing

2006

Andy Fairweather Low, *Sweet Soulful Music*; producer, engineer, mixing

2008

The Clash, *Live at Shea Stadium*; engineer

Ian McLagan & the Bump Band, *Never Say Never*; mastering, mixing

2011

Ryan Adams, *Ashes & Fire*; producer, engineer, mixing

Ben Waters, *Boogie 4 Stu: A Tribute to Ian Stewart*; mixing

2012

The Rolling Stones, *Charlie Is My Darling: Ireland 1965*; engineer

The Staves, *Dead & Born & Grown & Live*; co-producer, engineer, mixing

The Rolling Stones, *GRRR!*; mixing

Band of Horses, *Mirage Rock*; producer, engineer, mixing

Ethan Johns, *If Not Now Then When?*; mixing

2013

Aaron Neville, *My True Story*; mixing

Patty Griffin, *Silver Bell*; mixing

2014

Benmont Tench, *You Should Be So Lucky*; producer, engineer, mixing

INDEX

Page numbers in italics refer to photos.

CREDITS

Page 77: Photograph by Michael Cooper, © Michael Cooper Collection

Page 79: Photograph by Ethan Russell, © Ethan Russell

Page 92: Photograph by Bill Wyman, © Bill Wyman Archive

Page 96: Photographs by Gered Mankowitz, © Bowstir Ltd 2014/Mankowitz.com

Page 119: Photographs by Glyn Johns, © Glyn Johns

Page 121: Photograph by Ethan Russell, © Apple Corps Ltd

Page 138: Photograph by Ethan Russell, © Apple Corps Ltd

Page 146: Photographer unknown, © Glyn Johns

Page 193: Photograph by Bernie Leadon

Page 202: Photograph by Henry Diltz, © Henry Diltz Photography

Page 205: Photograph by Gered Mankowitz, © Bowstir Ltd 2014/Mankowitz.com

Page 221: Photographer unknown, © Bill Wyman Archive

Page 243: Photographs by Ethan Russell, © Ethan Russell

Page 253: Photograph by Glyn Johns, © Glyn Johns

Page 258: Photographs by Ian Stewart, © Ian Stewart Photographic Collection

Page 265: Photograph by Ian Stewart, © Ian Stewart Photographic Collection

Page 275: Photograph by Henry Diltz, © Henry Diltz Photography

Page 278: Photograph by Henry Diltz, © Henry Diltz Photography

Page 281: Photograph of Ryan Adams by Mandy Moore. Photograph of Norah Jones by Neal Casal

Page 282: Photograph by Christoper Wilson, © Christopher Wilson Photography

Page 284: Photograph by Julia Wick

ABOUT THE AUTHOR

Glyn Johns was the producer or engineer of a number of rock's classic albums, including those by The Rolling Stones, Eric Clapton, the Eagles, The Who, The Beatles, The Clash, and such singular artists as Joan Armatrading and Ryan Adams. He was inducted into the Rock and Roll Hall of Fame in 2012.